COMPREHENSIVE RESEARCH
AND STUDY GUIDE

BLOOM'S
MAJOR
DRAMATISTS

August
Wilson

EDITED AND WITH AN
INTRODUCTION BY HAROLD BLOOM

KT-524-463

BLOOM'S MAJOR DRAMATISTS

Aeschylus

Anton Chekhov

Aristophanes

Berthold Brecht

Euripides

Henrik Ibsen

Ben Johnson

Christopher Marlowe

Arthur Miller

Eugene O'Neill

Shakespeare's Comedies

Shakespeare's Histories

Shakespeare's Romances

Shakespeare's Tragedies

George Bernard Shaw

Neil Simon

Sophocles

Tennessee Williams

August Wilson

BLOOM'S MAJOR NOVELISTS

Jane Austen

The Brontës

Willa Cather

Stephen Crane

Charles Dickens

Fyodor Dostoevsky

William Faulkner

F. Scott Fitzgerald

Thomas Hardy

Nathaniel Hawthorne

Ernest Hemingway

Henry James

James Joyce

D. H. Lawrence

Toni Morrison

John Steinbeck

Stendhal

Leo Tolstoy

Mark Twain

Alice Walker

Edith Wharton

Virginia Woolf

BLOOM'S MAJOR WORLD POETS

Geoffrey Chaucer

Emily Dickinson

John Donne

T. S. Eliot

Robert Frost

Langston Hughes

John Milton

Edgar Allan Poe

Shakespeare's Poems & Sonnets

Alfred, Lord Tennyson

Walt Whitman

William Wordsworth

BLOOM'S MAJOR SHORT STORY WRITERS

William Faulkner

F. Scott Fitzgerald

Ernest Hemingway

O. Henry

James Joyce

Herman Melville

Flannery O'Connor

Edgar Allan Poe

J. D. Salinger

John Steinbeck

Mark Twain

Eudora Welty

COMPREHENSIVE RESEARCH
AND STUDY GUIDE

BLOOM'S
MAJOR
DRAMATISTS

August
Wilson

EDITED AND WITH AN INTRODUCTION
BY HAROLD BLOOM

BATH SPA UNIVERSITY
NEWTON PARK LIBRARY

Class No.

8 0 8 54 WIL B

Dawson 11 07

Bloom's Major Dramatists: August Wilson

Copyright © 2002 by Infobase Publishing
Introduction © 2002 by Harold Bloom

All rights reserved. No part of this publication may be reproduced or
utilized in any form or by any means, electronic or mechanical, including
photocopying, recording, or by any information storage or retrieval
systems, without permission in writing from the publisher. For more
information contact:

Chelsea House
An imprint of Infobase Publishing
132 West 31st Street
New York NY 10001

Library of Congress Cataloging-in-Publication Data
August Wilson / edited and with an introduction by Harold Bloom.
     p. cm. — (Bloom's major dramatists)
  Includes bibliographical references and index.
  ISBN 0-7910-6362-3 (alk. paper)
  1. Wilson, August—Criticism and interpretation. 2. Historical drama
American—History and criticism.   3. African Americans in literature.
I. Bloom, Harold. II. Series.

PS3573.I45677 Z955 2001
812'.54—dc21   2001042336

Chelsea House books are available at special discounts when purchased
in bulk quantities for businesses, associations, institutions, or sales
promotions. Please call our Special Sales Department in New York
at (212) 967-8800 or (800) 322-8755.

You can find Chelsea House on the World Wide Web at
http://www.chelseahouse.com

Contributing Editor: Anne Marie Albertazzi
Produced by: Robert Gerson Publisher's Services, Santa Barbara, CA

Printed in the United States of America

IBT 10 9 8 7 6 5 4 3

This book is printed on acid-free paper.

Contents

User's Guide   7

Editor's Note   8

Introduction   9

Biography of August Wilson   11

Plot Summary of *Ma Rainey's Black Bottom*   14

List of Characters in *Ma Rainey's Black Bottom*   17

Critical Views on *Ma Rainey's Black Bottom*

    James C. McKelly on the Marketability of Black Culture   20

    Eileen Crawford on the Play as Greek Tragedy   22

    Sandra Adell on Ma's and Levee's Black and White Loyalties   23

    Sandra G. Shannon on the Play as Blues Composition   25

    Kim Pereira on the Collision of Blues and Swing   26

    Harry J. Elam, Jr. on Ma Rainey's Sexuality   28

Plot Summary of *Fences*   30

List of Characters in *Fences*   34

Critical Views on *Fences*

    Christine Birdwell on Scenes as Innings   36

    Pamela Jean Monaco on the Spectre of Death   37

    John Timpane on Pre- and Post-War Athletics   39

    Sandra G. Shannon on Race Relations in the 1950s   40

    Peter Wolfe on the Strength of Troy   42

    Joseph H. Wessling on the Play as Metacomedy   43

    Anna S. Blumenthal on the Instructive Potential of Troy's Stories   45

Plot Summary of *Joe Turner's Come and Gone*   47

List of Characters in *Joe Turner's Come and Gone*   51

Critical Views on *Joe Turner's Come and Gone*

    Patricia Gantt on Southern Personalities in the Play   54

    Missy Dehn Kubitschek on Bertha's and Bynum's Shamanism   55

    Trudier Harris on Africanizing the Audience   57

    Douglas Anderson on Afro-Baptist and Biblical Sources for Bynum's Conversion Narrative   58

    Sandra G. Shannon on Shiny Man as Surrogate God   60

    Mary L. Bogumil on the Cultural and Etymological Origins of the Juba   61

Plot Summary of *Two Trains Running*   63

List of Characters in *Two Trains Running*   66

Critical Views on *Two Trains Running*

  Lisa Wilde on Chance and the Occult   68

  Kim Marra on Risa and Black Female Self-Hatred   69

  Mark William Rocha on Overhearing Holloway   71

  Sandra G. Shannon on the Legacy of Malcolm X   73

  Kim Pereira on the Symbolic Death of the Civil Rights Movement   74

  Qun Wang on Heroism in the Play   76

Works by August Wilson   79

Works about August Wilson   81

Index of Themes and Ideas   84

User's Guide

This volume is designed to present biographical, critical, and bibliographical information on the author's best-known or most important works. Following Harold Bloom's editor's note and introduction is a detailed biography of the author, discussing major life events and important literary accomplishments. A plot summary of each play follows, tracing significant themes, patterns, and motifs in the work.

A selection of critical extracts, derived from previously published material from leading critics, analyzes aspects of each play. The extracts consist of statements from the author, if available, early reviews of the work, and later evaluations up to the present. A bibliography of the author's writings (including a complete list of all works written, cowritten, edited, and translated), a list of additional books and articles on the author and his or her work, and an index of themes and ideas in the author's writings conclude the volume.

~

Harold Bloom is Sterling Professor of the Humanities at Yale University and Henry W. and Albert A. Berg Professor of English at the New York University Graduate School. He is the author of over 20 books, including *Shelley's Mythmaking* (1959), *The Visionary Company* (1961), *Blake's Apocalypse* (1963), *Yeats* (1970), *A Map of Misreading* (1975), *Kabbalah and Criticism* (1975), *Agon: Toward a Theory of Revisionism* (1982), *The American Religion* (1992), *The Western Canon* (1994), and *Omens of Millennium: The Gnosis of Angels, Dreams, and Resurrection* (1996). *The Anxiety of Influence* (1973) sets forth Professor Bloom's provocative theory of the literary relationships between the great writers and their predecessors. His most recent books include *Shakespeare: The Invention of the Human,* a 1998 National Book Award finalist, and *How to Read and Why,* which was published in 2000.

Professor Bloom earned his Ph.D. from Yale University in 1955 and has served on the Yale faculty since then. He is a 1985 MacArthur Foundation Award recipient, served as the Charles Eliot Norton Professor of Poetry at Harvard University in 1987–88, and has received honorary degrees from the universities of Rome and Bologna. In 1999, Professor Bloom received the prestigious American Academy of Arts and Letters Gold Medal for Criticism.

Currently, Harold Bloom is the editor of numerous Chelsea House volumes of literary criticism, including the series BLOOM'S NOTES, BLOOM'S MAJOR DRAMATISTS, BLOOM'S MAJOR NOVELISTS, MAJOR LITERARY CHARACTERS, MODERN CRITICAL VIEWS, MODERN CRITICAL INTERPRETATIONS, and WOMEN WRITERS OF ENGLISH AND THEIR WORKS.

Editor's Note

My Introduction centers upon what seems to me August Wilson's strongest achievement to date: *Joe Turner's Come and Gone* (1984), and emphasizes the play's religious intensities.

Ma Rainey's Black Bottom is viewed by James C. McKelly in its historical context of 1927 Chicago, where two African American cultures clash: rural southerners and urban northerners, while Eileen Crawford finds a tragic configuration governing the play. Sandra Adell studies the play's black-white clash of loyalties, after which Sandra G. Shannon locates the play's construction in the pattern of the Blues. For Kim Pereira, the collision of Blues and Swing is crucial to the play, while Harry J. Elam, Jr. relates Ma Rainey's independence as a singer to her lesbianism.

Fences, Troy Maxson's play (memorably portrayed by James Earl Jones) is analyzed by Christine Birdwell on the structural analogue of a baseball game, and by Pamela Jean Monaco as an allegory of death. For John Timpane, the crucial contrast is between waning racism in the transition to post-War America, while Sandra G. Shannon reminds us how vexed race relations were in the 1950s. Troy's psychic strength is studied by Peter Wolfe, after which Joseph H. Wessling explores the play's genre, and Anna S. Blumenthal admires Troy's teacherly storytelling.

The pain of recent slave pasts is explored as the background of *Joe Turner's* by Patricia Gantt, while Missy Dehn Kubitschek centers upon Bynum's African shamanism. For Trudier Harris, the play is a voyage to black realities for white audiences, after which Douglas Anderson uses the work of Michal Sobel to demonstrate an African-Baptist conversion pattern, in which "the little me in the big me" is activated, as it is by Bynum in Loomis. The Shiny Man figure is interpreted by Sandra G. Shannon as a critique of white visions of God. Mary L. Bogumil explains the Juba dance as a mode of spiritual healing.

For Lisa Wilde, the image of gambling is transmogrified by *Two Trains Running* into a liberating mode, while Kim Marra broods on the representation of black female self-hatred in the play. Mark William Rocha maintains that Wilson is preaching revolutionary continuity to young black Americans, after which Sandra G. Shannon and Kim Pereira find the end of the Civil Rights Crusade in Wilson's play. Qun Wang, not disagreeing, nevertheless exalts the drama's vision of black heroism.

Introduction

HAROLD BLOOM

I recall attending a performance of *Joe Turner's Come and Gone* at Yale in 1986, and came away more moved than I had been by *Ma Rainey's Black Bottom* and *Fences*. *Two Trains Running* I have never seen, and have just read for the first time, after rereading three earlier plays in the University of Pittsburgh Press's very useful *Three Plays* (1991), which has a stern Preface by the dramatist, and a useful Afterword by Paul Cater Harrison. Returning to the text of *Joe Turner's Come and Gone* after a decade is a remarkable experience in reading, since few plays by American dramatists hold up well away from the stage. As a literary work, *Joe Turner's Come and Gone* is authentically impressive, particularly in its spiritual insights. August Wilson's political stance as a black nationalist is present in *Joe Turner's* (to give it a short title), but his art as a dramatist surmounts the tendentiousness that elsewhere distracts me. Whether or not his other celebrated plays may prove to be period pieces (like those of Bullins and Baraka), I am uncertain, but there is a likely permanence in *Joe Turner's*, perhaps because of its profound depiction of the African American roots of what I have learned to call the American Religion, the actual faith of white Protestants in the United States.

The summer of 2001 is hardly a good time anyway to argue nationalist stances among African Americans, now that the full extent of black disenfranchisement in Jeb Bush's Florida is being revealed. It is clear that if there had been an unimpeded African American vote in Florida, the Supreme Court would not have been able to appoint George W. Bush as President. Since August Wilson's project is to compose a play for every decade of the black experience in twentieth century America, one wryly awaits what he might choose to do with the Florida Outrage of November 2000.

Wilson, in his Preface to *Three Plays*, offers a powerful reading of his masterwork:

> There is a moment in *Joe Turner's Come and Gone* at the end of the first act when the residents of the household, in an act of tribal solidarity and recognition of communal history, dance a Juba. Herald Loomis interrupts it to release a terrifying vision of bones walking on the water. From the outset he has been a man who has suffered a

spiritual dislocation and is searching for a world that contains his image. The years of bondage to Joe Turner have disrupted his life and severed his connection with his past. His vision is of bones walking on water that sink and wash up on the shore as fully fleshed humans. It is not the bones walking on the water that is the terrifying part of the vision—it is when they take on flesh and reveal themselves to be like him. "They black. Just like you and me. Ain't no difference." It is the shock of recognition that his birth has origins in the manifest act of the creator, that he is in fact akin to the gods. Somewhere in the Atlantic Ocean lie the bones of millions of Africans who died before reaching the New World. The flesh of their flesh populates the Americas from Mississippi to Montevideo. Loomis is made witness to the resurrection and restoration of these bones. He has only to reconcile this vision with his learned experiences and recognize he is one of the "bones people." At the end of the play he repudiates the idea that salvation comes from outside of himself and claims his moral personality by slashing his chest in a bloodletting rite that severs his bonds and demonstrates his willingness to bleed as an act of redemption.

Spiritually, this is both greatly suggestive and not unconfusing. Why does Loomis slash himself? There is a deep pattern of African gnosticism in the colonial black Baptists, who carried on from their heritage in affirming "the little me within the big me," the spark of the Alien God that was the best and oldest part of them, free of the Creation-Fall. Michal Sobel has shown how this pattern recurs in African American religion, and I suspect it was transmitted by the African Baptists to the original Southern Baptists. If Loomis slashes himself as a parody of and against Christian blood atonement, I could understand it more readily, but Wilson violates African tradition by the chest-slashing that is a bloodletting, bond-severing act of redemption. Perhaps Wilson felt he needed this self-violence as a dramatic gesture, and yet it may detract from the rebirth of Loomis. If this is a flaw, it is a small one in so strong a play. ✸

Biography of August Wilson

August Wilson was born Frederick August Kittel in 1945, the son of a white German immigrant baker named Frederick Kittel and a black woman whose maiden name was Daisy Wilson. He grew up in a two-room apartment in a Pittsburgh ghetto community called the Hill. His mother, abandoned by the father of her children, supported young August and his five siblings with welfare checks and janitorial wages. The only black child in a parochial school, August was the target of fierce racism. Reading from the age of four, he was accused in high school of plagiarizing a paper on Napoleon. Unable to pass the ninth grade as a result, he dropped out of school and began to rely solely on the public library and the streets for his education. In the library he educated himself by reading the works of African-American writers such as Langston Hughes, Ralph Ellison, Richard Wright, and Arna Bontemps. Aspiring to be a writer, Wilson studied the speech and behavior of people he encountered on the street. He also observed the people he met in his various jobs as porter, short-order cook, gardener, and dishwasher.

Wilson, who recalls that dropping out of school gave him the freedom to educate himself without censorship, began his career as a writer on April 1, 1965, when he bought a typewriter with the $20 he received for writing his sister's college term paper. In that same year, his biological father died and he changed his name to August Wilson. Small magazines such as *Black Lines* and *Black World* published some of Wilson's poems in 1971 and 1972. In the late 1960s and early 1970s, he co-founded Black Horizon on the Hill, a community theater. Through this theater, he participated in the activism of the Black Power movement and became committed to increasing political awareness in his community. Since that time, Wilson has considered himself a Black Nationalist.

Wilson's career leaped forward in 1978 when he was invited by his friend Claude Purdy to write plays for a black theater called Penumbra in St. Paul, Minnesota. He also wrote scripts for the Science Museum of Minnesota. Away from his home town, Wilson's ear for his native Pittsburgh dialect became even more finely tuned, and he began to write plays that reflected the sights and sounds of his old neighborhood. His first two plays, *Black Bart and the Sacred Hills* and *Jitney,* received little notice; but his third play, *Ma Rainey's Black Bottom,* received a staged reading at the National Playwright's Conference at the Eugene O'Neill Theater Center in Connecticut in 1981. There his play attracted the attention of Lloyd Richards, the artistic director for the Yale School of Drama, who helped Wilson revise it and proceeded to stage it at the Yale Repertory Theater in 1984. Later that year, *Ma Rainey's Black Bottom* opened at the Cort Theater on Broadway and ran for 275 performances. It won the New York Drama Critics Circle Award and several Tony Nominations.

Wilson's next play, *Fences,* won the Pulitzer Prize, a Tony award for best play, a New York Drama Critics Circle Award and an American Theatre Critics Award, all in 1987. It featured James Earl Jones as Troy Maxson. Following *Fences* came more award-winning and critically acclaimed plays: *Joe Turner's Come and Gone* received the New York Drama Critics Circle Award in 1988; *The Piano Lesson* received the 1990 Pulitzer Prize, the New York Drama Critics Circle Award, and the American Theatre Critics Award; *Two Trains Running* received the 1990 American Theatre Critics Award; and *Seven Guitars* won the 1996 New York Drama Critics Circle Award. August Wilson was the first African American playwright to have more than one play on Broadway simultaneously. In addition, he was named by *Post-Gazette* as the "top Pittsburgh cultural power broker" in 1999. Wilson has used his high visibility to become an outspoken advocate for African Americans.

King Hedley II, which is set in 1985, premiered at the Pittsburgh Public Theater in 1999. It has played in Seattle as well as at the Goodman Theater in Chicago. Most recently, it opened at the Kennedy Center in Washington, D.C. in March of 2001. Since *Ma Rainey,* all of Wilson's plays have debuted at the National Playwright's Conference, continued on to the Yale Repertory Theater and other regional theaters, then opened on Broadway. Almost all of Wilson's plays have been directed by Lloyd Richards, but more recently Wilson has worked with director Marion Isaac McClinton.

Each of August Wilson's eight plays offers a first-hand history of a decade in twentieth century American history from the 1910s to the 1980s, and each play takes up at least one major issue facing African Americans within that decade. *Joe Turner's Come and Gone,* for example, portrays the first generation of African Americans born free, while *Two Trains Running* depicts life after the death of Malcolm X and the civil rights movement. All Wilson's plays seem to share the preoccupation with uprootedness and feature characters who struggle to define themselves and their African heritage within the context of racism and slavery. Thus, August Wilson has been considered an enormously important cultural historian who gives an authentic voice to African Americans throughout twentieth century history. Wilson's critics agree that he has a remarkable talent for capturing the poetic cadence and rhythmic beats of his native Pittsburgh dialect. He has been praised as having a finely tuned ear for dialogue and linguistic rhythms. In addition, critics commend Wilson's ability to create stirring characters and draw upon African myths and folklore. While he has been compared to Arthur Miller, Tennessee Williams, and Eugene O'Neill, Wilson noted in a 1987 interview for the *New York Newsday* that his most important literary influence has been the blues: "I see the blues as a book of literature and it influences everything I do . . . Blacks' cultural response to the world is contained in the blues."

In 1999, August Wilson was honored at the 100th anniversary of the Hill District Branch Library, the very place in which he educated himself many years ago. Today, Wilson is the father of Azula Carmen by his present wife Constanza Romero, and Sakina Ansari Wilson by his first wife Brenda Burton. ❀

Plot Summary of
Ma Rainey's Black Bottom

The action of *Ma Rainey's Black Bottom* occurs in one afternoon at a Chicago recording studio in 1927. The main character is based on Ma Rainey, the 1920s recording star whose nickname was "Mother of the Blues." Some critics have viewed Ma Rainey as a victim of exploitation by the white recording industry, while others have pointed to how Ma exploits her own band and uses manipulation to keep her white employers as uncomfortable as possible. It is generally agreed, however, that all the black characters in this play tend to define themselves through their reactions to racism.

As **Act One** begins, Sturdyvant, the studio owner and Irvin, Ma's manager, prepare the mike for the recording session ahead. As the band members Cutler, Slow Drag, Toledo and Levee wait for Ma to arrive, we learn through their bantering how each has adapted to life. Cutler, the trombonist and band leader, simply defers to both Ma and the white man and wants others to do the same. Slow Drag, the bassist, drinks to escape. Toledo, the pianist, draws from his reading to make pseudo-intellectual pronouncements about life in a white world. Levee, the trumpeter, dissatisfied and combative with everyone, seeks artistic sovereignty through an elusive recording contract with Sturdyvant.

As the band rehearses Levee's version of Ma's song for the first time, it becomes clear that Levee's swing style is upstart and aggressive in relation to the old blues style. Just as his music creates friction, his personality causes rifts. He shuns Toledo's book knowledge and berates him as "the only cracker-talking nigger I know," bickers with Cutler over who is in charge of the band, snaps at Slow Drag for stepping on his shoes, and tells Toledo his shoes are ugly. He vows to sell his soul to the devil and angrily challenges God to strike him down for doing so.

Though there are no scene breaks, the action alternates between the band room and the recording studio. The band room showcases Levee's rash pugnacity and the studio showcases Ma's stubborn irascibility. Through this double staging, Wilson establishes the tension between Ma and Levee, a complex relationship of much interest to critics. Ma Rainey arrives accompanied by her nephew Sylvester, her lover Dussie Mae, and a policeman. Irvin, who prides himself on his skills of diplomacy between whites and blacks, pays off the policeman so that Ma will not be charged with assault and battery for an earlier altercation with a racist cab driver. Back in the band room, Slow Drag relates the story behind his name: he once won a slow drag contest dancing with another man's woman. Toledo compares the black man's history to the undesirable leftovers from the white man's great stew of history. As they rehearse, Ma, who is in the studio, hears Levee's version of Black Bottom and finds it distasteful, despite Irvin's insistence that this version will help her keep up with the new changes in music. Ma is stubbornly against the new sound; her ultimate authority is the voice inside her and the creativity that is in her own heart.

Levee's anger intensifies as he finds out that Ma's stuttering nephew will take over his part in performing the voice introduction to the song. Cutler, in his usual way, reminds Levee that Ma has the final say and the trumpeter can be replaced easily. Adding to Levee's frustration, Toledo says Levee is "spooked up by the white man" because he says "yessir" to Sturdyvant. Offended at the insinuation that he is an Uncle Tom, Levee bursts forth with a story from his childhood in which at age four he watched his mother being raped by a gang of white men. An ugly scar across his chest is the reminder of his fumbling attempts to defend his mother with a knife. His father, who was hung and burned for taking vengeance on the white men, had learned to smile in the face of his enemies. Levee, unknowingly participating in the racism that degrades him, wants to do the same.

At the beginning of **Act Two**, Levee protests to Ma about Sylvester's incompetence. Ma, dismissing him, has her own axe to grind. While Sturdyvant and Irvin may think her demands are petty, she insists that she be given every convenience in the studio because in truth she is treated as their whore. It is her voice, disembodied from her personhood, that the studio wants; and when they have captured it in a box, they no longer have any use for her. As she puts it "they rollover and put their pants on." Whites, Ma complains, do not understand the blues because they do not know the experience from which it emanates. Blues to her is a way of understanding life; it has always been around, even before her. As Ma carries on in the studio, Levee is flirting with and kissing Ma's lover Dussie Mae, whom Cutler has said is "out for what she can get."

After the performance of "Ma Rainey's Black Bottom," a song about a black clog dance popular in the 1920s, Sturdyvant realizes that it has not recorded properly. Levee is suspected of absent-mindedly kicking the microphone plug out of the wall. An angry Ma reluctantly agrees to wait fifteen minutes while the technical problems are resolved. In the meantime Toledo illustrates his theory that one must never be a fool twice by telling the story of his marriage. His wife joined the church after marrying him and left him one day because Toledo must have looked like a heathen compared to the men in church. Unlike Levee, he argues, he will not be the fool twice; he has learned from his mistakes. As for Levee's desire to sell his soul to the devil, Toledo claims he has already sold his soul by giving up who he is to become an imitation white man. These and other blunt criticisms only increase Levee's anger. Violence breaks out as Cutler attacks Levee for blaspheming his God; Levee retaliates by threatening him with a knife and then pointing the knife upward to challenge God himself.

Levee's anger and frustration increase when Ma fires him for talking back to her and Sturdyvant reneges on his promise to record the songs Levee wrote. Levee reaches the breaking point when Toledo accidentally steps on his shoes. He rushes at Toledo and stabs him in the back. It is the look in Toledo's eyes that tells him what he has done, and the guilt is so unbearable that he angrily orders Toledo to close his eyes, then appeals to Cutler to make him close them. Cutler only answers by sending for Mr. Irvin, and somewhere a muted trumpet's painful wail is heard as the lights go down. ❀

List of Characters in
Ma Rainey's Black Bottom

Sturdyvant is a music producer who records Ma Rainey's work. His relationship to black performers is governed by his fixation on money, and as stage directions tell us, he "prefers to deal with them at an arm's length." Sturdyvant relies on Irvin to keep Ma Rainey under control; her unpredictable and arrogant behavior undercuts efficiency in a way that makes him extremely anxious. Levee feels encouraged by him to write songs in the new swing style and form his own band, but in the end he denies Levee a chance at performing them.

Irvin is Ma Rainey's manager. He keeps things running smoothly at the studio by diplomatically balancing Ma's demands for special treatment with Sturdyvant's impatience and impersonal efficiency. Among other accommodations, he pays off the policeman who charges Ma with assault and battery so that she does not have to go to jail, and he keeps the band comfortable by offering sandwiches and words of encouragement.

Cutler is the leader of the band and plays the guitar and trombone. He tries to talk sense into the impetuous Levee, often reminding him that no matter how innovative and marketable Levee's musical creations might seem, he is merely the accompanist for Ma Rainey, who makes all the creative decisions. The conflict between Cutler and Levee reaches its peak when Levee blasphemes Cutler's God by saying he is a white man's God. Cutler furiously punches Levee, who retaliates by waving his knife in the air, challenging Cutler's God to a fight. After Levee stabs Toledo, Cutler in his usual fashion defers to the white man to handle the situation.

Toledo is the one member of the group who can read and he tends to use his eclectic knowledge to make sense of life. His insight, a combination of life experience and intellectual dilettantism, leads him to describe the black man as leftovers from the white man's historical stew, and to surmise that the black man is the creator of his own dissatisfaction. His observations often point up some foolishness on the part of Levee, who clashes with him often and with increasing intensity as the play goes on. Finally Levee stabs him for stepping on his shoes, signifying both the intensity of Levee's accumulated anger and Toledo's superior ability to provoke it.

Slow Drag is the bass player. He gets his name from a time when he won a slow drag dance contest by dancing with another man's woman. His great achievement was convincing the other man he was doing him a favor, while never missing a beat on the dance floor. Thus despite his bored appearance he is quite crafty and intelligent. Slow Drag enjoys his bourbon, taking nips of it often as a way of getting through the day.

Levee is a trumpet player in his early thirties, about twenty years younger than the rest of the players. Being of a new generation, he is irritated and restless about having to play what he considers "jug band" music. He dreams of starting a band of his own and performing a more energetic style of music that will excite young people. His anger seems to stem from having witnessed his mother raped by a gang of white men when he was eight. That anger finally explodes when Sturdyvant rejects his new music, leading him to stab Toledo for stepping on his shoes.

Ma Rainey is a character based on the actual 1920s blues artist of the same name (Gertrude "Ma" Rainey, or "The Mother of the Blues"). However, Wilson has fictionalized her. She has been in the music business since she was a young girl and has built up not only a fan base but a tough exterior. Her primary creative authority is her own intuition, or what is inside her heart; it is clear she has not been able to depend on anyone but herself all these years. Ma will not be pushed around or controlled by Sturdyvant, nor by her own band, snatching at any autonomy she can get in a world where the black performer is merely the white producer's whore.

The Policeman brings Ma and her entourage into the studio to give Irvin a chance to pay him off before he takes her to jail for assault and battery. He is exasperated with Ma but sees her as an opportunity to receive some extra cash. Irvin obliges, and the policeman, another white man cashing in on discrimination, leaves with a good-natured wink.

Dussie Mae is Ma Rainey's lover. She is a kept woman who wears nice dresses and does not have to worry about money, but her sexuality cannot be contained for long and her eye wanders to Levee. She is smart enough not to get stuck with a man like Levee who could never support her well, but she gives in to Levee's advances when she is sure Ma cannot see her.

Sylvester is Ma's nephew. He has a stutter that makes him defensive. Levee taunts him, and the other band members want to do the song without him. However, Ma's stubborn determination to see the talent in him gives him the courage to perform the voice introduction to her song flawlessly after a few takes. ❀

Critical Views on
Ma Rainey's Black Bottom

JAMES C. MCKELLY ON THE MARKETABILITY OF
BLACK CULTURE

[James C. McKelly teaches English at Auburn University.
His work appears in numerous scholarly journals, including
African American Review, The Eugene O'Neill Newsletter, and
Profession. In this excerpt McKelly reveals how Sturdyvant's
recording studio reflects socioeconomic hierarchies in the
late 1920s.]

The action of August Wilson's 1981 *Ma Rainey's Black Bottom* takes
place on a historical cusp, in the contradictory context of an era
both dominated by stolid cultural hierarchies and turbulent with
sociological transition. Wilson sets the play in 1927 Chicago, a nexus
volatile with the increasing admixture of two distinct African-American cultures: displaced rural southerners and ghettoized urban
northerners. In *Specifying,* Susan Willis proposes that Toni Morrison
"develops the social and psychological aspects that characterize the
lived experience of [this] cultural transition"; in *Ma Rainey,* Wilson
explores the consequences of these social and psychological tensions
in the realm of the aesthetic. The musical artist of the period, of
which Wilson's central characters are potently representative types, is
challenged by the emerging issues of artistic direction forced by this
cultural ambiguity: whether to continue to compose and perform
music that confirms and enriches a southern tradition, thereby
serving both nostalgia and authenticity, or to devote energy and
vision to a more urban, contemporary evolution of the form,
thereby serving relevance and currency. According to Willis, the
problem at the center of Morrison's writing is "how to maintain an
Afro-American cultural heritage once the relationship to the black
rural South has been stretched thin over distance and generations."
In *Ma Rainey,* Wilson examines not only the question of how the gift
of the past can bequeath itself to the present, but of whether it is
possible for the future to flourish under the burden of this heritage.

Hovering like a ghost over this internal debate over black cultural
integrity is the ineluctable fact of white majority oppression. The

systemic inequity manifests itself in the life of the musical artist on two levels. The first is broadly socioeconomic. The technologies essential to the production and distribution of any work of art that is to survive on the mass market are in the hands of members of the dominant culture. Even if the market is primarily black, as it is for the artists in *Ma Rainey,* white owners and administrators control all access to it. Secondly, on a more personally aesthetic level, for the white key-holders of mass technology, art is no more than product, the artist no more than labor. As a result, the issues of artistic direction, tone, structure, and import which are of crucial importance to the artist are germane to the concerns of the owners only in so far as they affect commercial considerations. Artists are empowered only to the degree that the product of their labor is a potential moneymaker. The only criterion for artistic quality and respect for the artist is marketability.

Wilson's set, a recording studio, provides a physical structure that is the symbolic embodiment of these hierarchies within which nascent African-American artistic production must fight for birth. The lowest rung in the studio ladder, in the basement of the building, is the band room, where the players can relax between sessions. The players may speak and act freely there, but their words and deeds, relegated to a realm where they are unseen and unheard, can have no unmediated or untrammeled affect upon production or performance decisions. The studio itself, on a level above the band room, is Ma's turf, where the material and arrangements played by the band must suit her, and where she demands the respect of the producer, if she is to perform. Above the studio, accessible by a spiral staircase, is the control room, in which the technology of the recording process is kept and manipulated, without which the sessions cannot be reproduced. The aloof quality of the control booth is accentuated by the fact that a horn is its only means of communication with the performers, emblematic of a remote, disembodied authority that, though it hears all, can be approached only through an intermediary. It is as if the very walls and stairs of the studio themselves are concrete extensions of the abstract sociocultural forces that govern the development and progression of minority art.

—James C. McKelly, "Hymns of Sedition: Portraits of the Artist in Contemporary African-American Drama," *Arizona Quarterly* 48, no. 1 (Spring 1992): pp. 87–107.

EILEEN CRAWFORD ON THE PLAY AS GREEK TRAGEDY

[Eileen Crawford is an Assistant Professor of English and Director of the Honors Program at the University of the District of Columbia, where she established a program in African and African-American Studies. Her work has been published in scholarly journals such as the *Journal of Black Studies* and the *College Language Association.* In this excerpt, Crawford explains how the play follows the conventions of Greek tragedy.]

August Wilson so designs this drama that it is Greek in its tragic configuration. The tragic moment occurs within the unities of time, place and action. The audience is well prepared for a death; all has moved toward that end. The question is whose? Both Ma Rainey and Toledo are of sufficient stature to talk of tragic dimensions, replete as they are with their individual indicators of hubris and a perceived loss of dignity. There will be no real recognition scene, however. The real figure with tragic potential is, of course, Ma Rainey. Given her historical status, however, Wilson cannot allow the drama to yield to the inevitable. Instead Wilson wisely focuses on the single motivation of Ma Rainey, Toledo, and Levee: the concern with the direction of one's artistic life and how to use this art of the blues to inform that life. Thus Wilson's characters are myopically disposed toward pushing their fate to the brink of disaster due to their personalities. For instance, Ma Rainey is a bragging, difficult woman quite capable of bringing tragedy to other people's lives. Additionally, she is independent, sexually adventurous, and refuses to be intimidated by her lack of formal education. As she says, "I have my own way of doing things." On the other hand, Levee's method of decoding the racial messages given by whites, like the other members of the band, is to engage in primal screams down the laughing barrel of anger, rage and dignity. Slow Drag determines to hid his innate intelligence for profitability and protection, while Cutler deals with the here and now, expecting and asking for nothing and getting out of life what little he can. This essential accommodation by all except Ma will ultimately prove the group's undoing. It becomes, then, a group loss, the black community's tragedy at the loss of an historical tradition. When Cutler reminds Levee that in his just-concluded subversion of Ma's song to the interests of Sturdyvant, he reminds Levee that he has been unnecessarily obsequious. Cutler continues, "You talking out your hat—that man comes in here, call you a boy, tell you to get off your ass and rehearse, and you can't say nothing to him, except Yessir!"; he has in his characteristic fashion unknowingly provoked the final incident.

—Eileen Crawford, "The B♭ Burden: The Invisibility of Ma Rainey's Black Bottom," *August Wilson: A Casebook,* ed. Marylin Elkins (New York and London: Garland Publishing, 1994): pp. 31–48.

SANDRA ADELL ON MA'S AND LEVEE'S BLACK AND WHITE LOYALTIES

[Associate Professor in the department of Afro-American Studies at the University of Wisconsin, Madison, Sandra Adell is the author of *Double-Consciousness/Double Bind: Theoretical Issues in Twentieth-Century Black Literature.* In this excerpt, Adell argues that Levee's misplaced reliance on the white man contrasts with Ma Rainey's loyalty to her own race.]

Levee wants to be like Ma Rainey. He believes that the white men respect her and that all he has to do to make them respect him is to turn over a good profit. Yet unlike Ma Rainey, who knows that it was black people and not white people who made her a star, Levee relies on Irvin and Sturdyvant to give him his break. Ma Rainey, on the other hand, has learned, after long years of performing on the Southern circuit, how to manipulate the powers that be. She has also learned to place a higher value on the blues tradition and all that it implies than on its technical innovations and mechanical reproduction. For example, when Irvin balks about not having enough time to let her stuttering nephew Sylvester record the lead-in lines to her "Black Bottom Blues," Ma Rainey does not hesitate to remind him that this recording session is something she does not need to do. She can easily return to her Southern tour, where over the years she has cultivated large numbers of loyal fans:

> If you wanna make a record, you gonna find time. I ain't playing with you, Irvin. I can walk out of here and go back

to my tour. I got plenty fans. I don't need to go through all of this. Just go and get the boy a microphone.

Ma Rainey doesn't need to go through the performance-inhibiting ordeal of a recording session because she remains solidly grounded in the tradition out of which her music evolved. Her *contract* is not with Irvin and Sturdyvant; it is with the people, the down-home folk who identify most closely with her brand of the blues. Her "Black Bottom" belongs to them, and she refuses to give it up to anyone else unless she gets something in return. As the last line of her "Moonshine Blues" goes, "You got to fetch it with you when you come." And when Irvin comes out of the control booth after the recording session with Sturdyvant's crooked deal to pay Sylvester with part of the money he owes her, Ma Rainey sends Irvin right back to fetch the boy's pay, then makes him and Sturdyvant beg her to sign the release forms.

> *Sturdyvant:* Hey, Ma . . . come on, sign the forms, huh?
> *Irvin:* Ma . . . come on now.
> *Ma Rainey:* Get your coat, Sylvester. Irvin, where's my car?
> *Irvin:* It's right out front, Ma. Here . . . I got the keys right here. Come on, sign the forms, huh?
> *Ma Rainey:* Irvin, give me my car keys!.
> *Irvin:* Sure, Ma . . . just sign the forms, huh?
> (*He gives her the keys, expecting a trade-off.*)
> *Ma Rainey:* Send them to my address and I'll get around to them.
> *Irvin:* Come on, Ma . . . I took care of everything, right? I straightened everything out.

Ma Rainey signs. Just before she makes her exit she signs, but by that time she has gotten everything she can out of Irvin and Sturdyvant and their recording machines, including the satisfaction of making them put everything on hold, of making them wait.

—Sandra Adell, "Speaking of Ma Rainey / Talking About the Blues," *May All Your Fences Have Gates: Essays on the Drama of August Wilson*, ed. Alan Nadel (Iowa City: University of Iowa Press, 1994): pp. 51–66.

SANDRA G. SHANNON ON THE PLAY AS BLUES COMPOSITION

[Sandra G. Shannon, Professor of English at Howard University, is the author of *The Dramatic Vision of August Wilson* and numerous scholarly articles on both Wilson and Amiri Baraka. In this excerpt, Shannon compares the play to a blues song.]

If regarded as a blues composition presented as a play, *Ma Rainey's Black Bottom* becomes infinitely more understandable. Like a blues song or jazz rendition, the play is a slow-building, repetitious, unpredictable ride on an emotional roller coaster. Ma does not appear until well into Act I, yet the goings-on during the prerehearsal session are analogous to a lengthy musical prelude leading up to the vocal accompaniment. Levee's recurring complaints against Ma and the other band-members functions as the refrain to this blues play; and the competing stories of Ma and her band echo the interwoven improvisations of blues and jazz performers. Corresponding to the emotion-charged lyrics of the blues song are the characters' tortured testimonies of survival. Both Ma and Levee, though constantly at odds with each other, at some point in the play turn inward to reveal the source of their private pain.

Although the blues dominates every aspect of *Ma Rainey's Black Bottom,* also at work in the play are a number of other identifiable elements of African American culture. Either directly or indirectly, some combination of the following themes runs through this and each of Wilson's subsequent plays: black people's need to establish and maintain ties with their immediate families as well as with their cultural ancestors; their mistaken devaluation of their own culture, prompted by a massive exodus from South to North after their emancipation; their heroic struggles and degrading compromises made to achieve economic stability; and the deterioration of their moral, spiritual, and familial values resulting from those compromises and that self-devaluation. To convey each of these major issues effectively in his work, Wilson continues to draw upon the dynamics of the blues, concerned that his audiences—especially the black members—explore both the emotional and historical dimensions of his work and see themselves in the process.

One of the most consistent of these cultural elements surfacing in *Ma Rainey* is what Paul Carter Harrison refers to as "the potency of the African continuum as a psychic and spiritual repository of values and survival strategies." In *Ma Rainey's Black Bottom,* this theme emerges indirectly in the comments made by the self-educated, pseudophilosopher Toledo; in the symbolic polarizations in the band's attitudes toward northern sophistication and southern naïveté, and, ultimately, in the vicious dispute between Levee and Ma Rainey over her "old jug band music" and his more modern, more danceable versions. Yet in the play representations of the African continuum in the play draw harsh criticism and denial from the black men in Ma's band rather than acknowledgment and reverence. To most of them Africa, like life in the South, is a distant world of painful memories and associations; any true measure of advancement, in their view, depends upon how un-African or how unsouthern they have become.

> —Sandra G. Shannon, *The Dramatic Vision of August Wilson* (Washington, D.C.: Howard University Press, 1995): pp. 77–79.

KIM PEREIRA ON THE COLLISION OF BLUES AND SWING

[Associate Professor of Acting and Dramatic Literature at Illinois State University, Kim Pereira is the author of *August Wilson and the African-American Odyssey.* In this excerpt, Pereira discusses the evolution of black music in 1927 from blues to swing and its significance in the play.]

Throughout the twentieth century black music has been in a continuous state of evolution, with a new mode of expression marking virtually every decade. There were the additive rhythms of ragtime; the twelve-bar call and response of the blues; jazz, swing, and the big band; be-bop and dazzling virtuosity; and fusion and the marriage of acoustic and electronic instruments. And, just when it seemed that the only possibilities were a reworking of old styles, rap emerged with its hard, driving rhythms, staccato vocals that simulated electronic voices, dance movements at once fluid and robotic, and lyrics that recalled the blues in their cries of protest.

In 1927, black music took one of these major leaps. The Harlem Renaissance was in its tenth year, and black musicians were gaining wide popularity after King Oliver's historic recording session four years earlier in 1923. In this same year, Duke Ellington launched his legendary Cotton Club engagement in Harlem, Count Basie embarked on his Kansas City career, and Louis Armstrong emerged from the shadow of Oliver's band with his "Hot Five" and "Hot Seven" recordings. Jazz was poised on the threshold of a new sound and a new era—swing and the big band.

It is in this changing era that Wilson sets his play *Ma Rainey's Black Bottom*, which takes place in a studio in Chicago in 1927 during a recording session by the blues singer Ma Rainey and her four black musician sidemen. The significance of this date echoes strongly through the play, for much of the action flows from a conflict between proponents of the old and new forms of black music: between the blues and swing.

Wilson clearly sketches this division early in the play through the stage directions accompanying the entrances of the characters. He draws a sharp distinction between the three older sidemen—Cutler, Toledo, and Slow Drag—and the younger Levee. Cutler, the trombonist and guitar player, is the "most sensible," with a playing style that is "solid and almost totally unembellished"; Toledo, the pianist, "recognizes that [his instrument's] limitations are an extension of himself" and "his insights are thought-provoking"; and Slow Drag, the bassist, is "deceptively intelligent, though, as his name implies, he appears to be slow." Levee is more flamboyant and "somewhat of a buffoon," with a "rakish and bright" temper and strident voice. Their personalities also reflect their attitudes toward music: the older three favor the more plaintive, deeply emotional sounds of the blues; Levee, the flashier rhythms of swing.

As he unfolds the events in the play and reveals the characters' stories of their past experiences, Wilson affords us glimpses into the development of their personalities and allows us to be privy to their efforts to survive the social and economic injustices that beset blacks in the early part of the twentieth century. Since music is an integral part of the lives and racial identity of these characters, much of the conflict centers around their music. The clash of the characters' personalities reflects the struggle for self-affirmation that blacks faced in the late 1920s.

—Kim Pereira, *August Wilson and the African-American Odyssey* (Urbana and Chicago: University of Illinois Press, 1995): pp. 13–14.

HARRY J. ELAM, JR. ON MA RAINEY'S SEXUALITY

[Harry J. Elam, Jr. teaches in the Stanford University Drama Department. He is a Christensen Professor for the Humanities, Director of the Committee on Black Performing Arts and Director of the Area One Program. He is the author of *Taking It to the Streets: The Social Protest Theater of Luis Valdez* and co-editor of *Colored Contradictions: An Anthology of Contemporary African American Drama*. In this excerpt, Elam discusses Ma Rainey's unconventional sexuality as commensurate to her blues style.]

Through the activity of singing the blues, Black women such as Ma Rainey positively acknowledged and represented black women's sexuality. Ma Rainey's songs displayed an earthy and forthright, crude and sassy sensuality. As she asserted control over the content and form of her songs, she equally declared control over her own sexuality. "She is in the moment of performance the primary subject of her own being. Her sexuality is precisely the physical expression of the highest self-regard and, often, the sheer pleasure she takes in her own powers" ("Interstices: A Small Drama of Words"). Present always in Ma Rainey's performance of her music was the concept of the black woman as empowered subject.

In her personal sex life as well as in her music and on stage performances, Ma Rainey refused to conform to traditional gender expectations. She was a bisexual with acknowledged lesbian relationships. According to Harrison, "Rainey's and Bessie Smith's episodes with women lovers are indicative of the independent stance they and other blues singers took on issues of personal choice" (*Black Pearls*).

Her lesbianism and the public knowledge of it further testified to Ma Rainey's personal revolt against male hegemony and her ability to survive outside male domination and societal norms.

Paradoxically, while Ma Rainey's own activities in life attempted to subvert the male dominated, heterosexual status quo, the events of Wilson's play appear to uphold it. Decidedly more overt than the physical exchanges between Ma and Dussie Mae, her younger lesbian or bi-sexual companion, is the sexual embrace shared by Dussie Mae and the young rebellious trumpet player, Levee. Protected by the privacy of the downstairs band room, they exchange a passionate kiss. Their stolen embrace emphasizes Levee's fateful defiance of Ma's authority. Significantly, Dussie Mae jeopardizes her financially stable—Ma has supplied her with money and clothing—but non-traditional lesbian relationship with Ma Rainey for an extremely tenuous but conventional heterosexual affair with Levee. Implicit is the message that relationships with men are more valuable.

—Harry J. Elam, Jr., "*Ma Rainey's Black Bottom:* Singing Wilson's Blues," *American Drama* 5, no. 2 (Spring 1996): pp. 76–99.

Plot Summary of
Fences

Fences has attracted much critical attention for its portrayal of the social and psychological effects of discrimination against black athletes. Troy Maxson and his son Cory represent the generations before and after integration of blacks into professional sports. Troy Maxson, a former baseball player who was overlooked by professional leagues because he was black, is now a disgruntled middle-aged garbage man. His son Cory, on the other hand, has been offered a college football scholarship and shows ostensible promise in the new world of Jackie Robinson and the eroding color barrier. Troy's merciless mistreatment of his family, borne of a deep-seated anger at a racist world and a dictatorial father, is complicated by his tragic loneliness in the face of death and his often genuinely good intentions. Because his character resists classification, he has fascinated many contemporary critics.

Set in 1957, all the action of *Fences* takes place in the front of Troy Maxson's house. **Act One, Scene One** begins as Troy and Jim Bono, fellow garbage collectors and longtime buddies, enjoy a drink on payday. The desultory talk between Troy, Bono, and Troy's wife Rose on this Friday evening hints at nascent conflicts that will erupt as the plot unfolds. Troy has filed a complaint with the union because blacks are never allowed to drive the garbage trucks. Bono nudges Troy for making eyes at another woman named Alberta. A failed baseball player, Troy gripes that the college football recruiters pursuing his son are hawking a lie because the black man never gets a fair chance in sports. Finally, Troy tells a story of three days and nights in 1941 when, suffering from pneumonia, he "wrassled" with Death and came out a winner. Since then he keeps ever vigilant against this personified Death, figured in his mind as a grinning, sickle-bearing foe.

At breakfast the next day (**Scene Two**), Rose and Troy are visited by Gabriel, Troy's younger brother whose World War II injury has left him with a plate in his head and an unshakeable conviction that he is the archangel Gabriel in league with Saint Peter. Once a tenant of Troy's, he has now taken a room at Miss Pearl's. Troy's displeasure at Gabriel's move probably stems from guilt, since the only way Troy was able to buy his house was to take the $3,000 the government gave Gabriel for his injury.

Four hours later, in **Scene Three,** an inebriated Troy returns home from drinking at Taylor's, the local bar. He belittles Cory's ambition to be recruited into college football and forbids him to play if it interferes with his job at the A&P. Troy, who says he was rejected by the professional leagues because of the color of his skin, claims his motive for discouraging his son is to prevent him from the pain of discrimination. Rose, however, reminds Troy that he was simply too old to play professionally by the time baseball became integrated.

Scene Four takes place on Friday two weeks later. Troy has been promoted to become the first black garbage truck driver. Rose urges Troy to sign the college recruitment papers but Troy is resentful that the boy has lied to him about quitting his job. To an audience including Rose, Lyons, Bono, and Gabe, Troy describes the day he first stopped being afraid of his father. When he was fourteen, he was whipped by his father for being with a girl, but when he realized that his father had whipped him out of jealousy, he lost respect for him and whipped him back.

Cory returns from discovering that Troy has told his football coach to send the recruiter away. He bitterly accuses his father of jealousy. For this insult, Troy calls strike one, warning his son that he had better not strike out.

Act Two begins the following morning. In **Scene One,** Bono criticizes Troy for having an affair with Alberta and encourages him to finish building the fence Rose has requested. Bono explains that some people build fences to keep people out while others build fences to keep people in. In this play, fences suggest both the racial barriers that kept Troy and other blacks out of professional sports and the various walls that Troy erects to shield himself from pain. For Bono, who promises that as soon as Troy finishes building the fence, he will buy his wife Lucille a refrigerator, the fence represents a scheme to get Troy to stay away from Alberta.

After Bono leaves, Troy tells Rose that Alberta is pregnant with his child. Troy explains that Alberta makes him feel different and takes him from the pressures and problems of his life. Rose retorts that she too has had dreams of something better, but she has buried those dreams in him and left them there, even though what she planted never bloomed. Angered, Troy grabs Rose's arm. Hearing Rose's protestations, Cory enters and manages to knock Troy to the ground. Troy calls strike two on his son and warns him not to strike out.

Scene Two takes place six months later. Rose is fed up with Troy's double dealing. He sneaks around after work, he has secretly signed release papers to put Gabe in the hospital and receive half of his paycheck, and he has refused to sign Cory's recruitment papers, effectively ending the boy's football career. The hospital calls to notify Troy that his baby has been delivered but Alberta has died in childbirth. Barely containing his rage, Troy directs it at Death, his longtime foe. Troy orders Death to come at him man to man next time, and to leave other people out of it. In the meantime, Death had better stay on the outside of the fence he will build around the yard.

Scene Three takes place three days later. Troy shows up with Alberta's baby, asking Rose if she will take care of the helpless child. Rose assents because she believes, ironically, that "you can't visit the sins of the father upon the child." Yet she makes it clear that she is in no way obligated to Troy himself. Troy from this point forward, she says, will be a "womanless man."

In **Scene Four,** two months later, Troy has insulated himself almost completely. An estranged Bono visits for a brief conversation in which Troy, drinking heavily, admits he is lonely being a driver because he has no one with whom to talk. Since Troy finished the fence, Bono kept up his end of the bargain by buying Lucille her refrigerator. When Bono leaves, Cory returns and begins to argue with his father. He taunts Troy for being a drunk who is jealous of his son. He wields a baseball bat against Troy but is afraid to use it; Troy easily takes the bat away and drives Cory off the yard. Cory has struck out.

Alone and desperate, Troy challenges Death to another fight. As the critic Pamela Jean Monaco argues, each appearance of Death in this play signifies the end of a relationship ("Father, Son, and Holy Ghost," p. 98). Just as Troy has summoned Death after the passing of Alberta, he beckons Death to register the loss of his son.

In **Scene Five,** which takes place in 1965, all are gathered at the house for Troy's funeral. Raynell, the child of Alberta and Troy, is now a young girl, Cory is a marine corporal, and Lyons, Troy's son by an earlier marriage, is serving out a sentence at the workhouse for cashing other people's checks. Rose relates that Troy died swinging the bat at the tree.

Cory announces to his mother that he will not go to the funeral because he wants just once to say no to his father. He sees his father as "That shadow digging into your flesh"; it is a shadow that he cannot shake off, and he hopes to distinguish himself from his father once and for all. Rose tells Cory he cannot escape the Troy that is within him, and that the shadow is himself. The play ends as Gabriel announces to Rose that he will tell St. Peter to open the gates of heaven. For the first time, Troy does not have to muscle his way past a barrier to get by; the passageway is free and clear. ❀

List of Characters in
Fences

Troy Maxson is a garbage collector. His faults are many: telling tall tales, drinking too much, womanizing, and mistreating his family. Yet, as Rose aptly describes him, he means to do more good than harm. Troy is obsessed with the figure of Death, an imaginary personification he rages at when drunk. A failed baseball player, he resents that his son has a chance to be recruited for college football and refuses to sign his consent forms. He dies in the act of swinging his bat.

Jim Bono, who met Troy in jail, is Troy's best friend, co-worker and admirer. He believes he has learned the best of what he knows from Troy, and appreciates him accordingly. Bono eventually becomes estranged from Troy because the latter's promotion separates them. Bono disapproves of Troy's infidelity but is unsuccessful at convincing him to stop seeing Alberta.

Rose is Troy's wife. She is devoted to Troy despite his faults, since he has given her a home and takes care of his responsibilities. A pragmatist, she corrects him when he tells lies or mistreats his friends and family, but ultimately she cannot prevent him from alienating his son and herself with his cruel behavior. After Troy reveals that he has a son by another woman, Rose will not let Troy back into her bed, yet she agrees to raise the child, who provides her with hope after Troy's death.

Lyons is Troy's son from a previous marriage. At 34 years old, he plays in a band and lives the life of a musician, though not a successful one. His relationship with Troy is confined mostly to borrowing money and taking criticism from him.

Gabriel is Troy's younger brother. Shot during World War II, he now has a steel plate in his head. As a result, he lives under a psychotic illusion that he is the archangel Gabriel who works side by side with Saint Peter in Heaven. Troy has used Gabe's settlement from the government to buy his house, in which Gabe once boarded. After Troy's death, Gabe believes he has opened the gates of heaven for him.

Cory is the son of Troy and Rose. His dream is to be a football player and his talent has attracted college recruiters. When Troy refuses to sign the recruitment papers, Cory is devastated and accuses his father of being jealous. Though he is angry, he cannot defend himself against his father and leaves home to join the Marines. He describes his father as "that shadow digging into your flesh" (II.v) and despite his efforts to escape, cannot shake off that part of Troy that will always plague him.

Raynell is the daughter of Troy and Alberta, raised by Rose. She is the symbol of the "sins of the father" but her innocence stands out as a beam of hope at the end of Troy's troubled and often wretched life. ✸

Critical Views on
Fences

CHRISTINE BIRDWELL ON SCENES AS INNINGS

[Christine Birdwell is an Associate Professor in Michigan State University's Department of American Thought and Language. In this excerpt, Birdwell notes the ways in which the dynamics of a baseball game inform the structure of Wilson's play.]

The fences of the title are both real and metaphorical, both defenses and obstructions. They are the backyard fence that Troy's wife wants him to build to improve the property and protect the family; they are the fences that enclose mental hospitals; they are the boundaries of graveyards but also of heaven (entered by St. Peter's gate). More importantly, they are family responsibilities and divisions between generations. They are *not* the white picket fences in the front yards of American Dream homes. Instead they are racial barriers keeping blacks, even great hitters who can slam balls over any ballpark fence, from realizing their potential.

In spite of the fact that *Fences'* protagonist was once such an athlete, the play is not solely about baseball in the sense or to the degree that films like *Bingo Long* or *Eight Men Out* are. *Fences'* milieu is not the sporting life. The images and rhythms of the play's language come as much from oral tradition and the blues as from playing field and locker room, and Troy Maxson's actions are not all the result of his experience with sports. But August Wilson does use baseball's forms and language to carry part of the meaning of his play. For example, the game's structure is the play's structure: nine scenes, like innings, from the seasons in the life of the hero. Troy has been an Alabama farm boy, a fourteen-year-old runaway, a poverty-stricken thief, a prison inmate, and—at the high point of his life—a great hitter. At the play's beginning—or first inning—it is 1957, and Troy at age fifty-three is now a hauler of garbage in a "middle American urban industrial city" (Richards in Wilson vii) never directly named but almost certainly Wilson's own hometown of Pittsburgh, Pennsylvania. The backyard and porch of Troy's inner city house have become his ballpark where, as the hard-working, responsible start of his home team, he is the husband, father, brother, lover, and storyteller who defies Death. At the play's end or ninth inning, it is 1965, and Troy is dead. On the morning of his funeral his family and his friend join to memorialize his losses and his wins.

During the other innings—a series of reminiscences, tall tales, and confrontations—Wilson tells us about Troy's relationship with his father, a sharecropper trapped in poverty who brutalized his family. We also witness Troy's interactions with Bono, a companion from prison days; with his loved and loving wife Rose and his war-wounded, deranged brother Gabriel (who believes himself to be the Archangel); and with his sons, Lyons by his first wife and Cory by Rose. We discover his affair with Alberta from Tallahassee, the mother of his daughter Raynell. We see Troy's hard-won "little victories" (Richards in Wilson viii) for his family—providing food for their stomachs, a roof over their heads, and clothes on their backs. We see his successful effort to challenge the city's garbage disposal system—"the white mens driving and the colored lifting"—by becoming a garbage truck driver instead of a trash lifter. But we also see his defeats: his continuing misunderstandings with Lyons, his institutionalizing of Gabriel, his estrangement from Bono, his loss of Alberta in childbirth, his alienation from Rose, and his broken kinship with Cory.

—Christine Birdwell, "Death as a Fastball on the Outside Corner: *Fences*' Troy Maxson and the American Dream," *Aethlon: The Journal of Sport Literature* 8, no. 1 (Fall 1990): pp. 87–96.

Pamela Jean Monaco on the Spectre of Death

[In this excerpt, Monaco discusses the significance of Death as a reminder of Troy's past.]

Like *Joe Turner's Come and Gone* and *The Piano Lesson*, *Fences* also contains an unseen presence that haunts the protagonist. The difference between this play and the other two is that this presence never is experienced by the audience. Even through we do not see the specters in the two earlier plays, their presence was made tangible for us because of the dramatic reactions of the other characters. In *Fences* the unseen presence is that of Death, which Troy reports to us and the other characters.

Troy "encounters" the presence of Death three times during the course of the play. The first time we hear of this specter is when Troy tells Bono of his encounter when he had pneumonia, which taught him that "I got to keep watch." The two other occurrences are not reported but happen when Troy stands alone on stage and speaks directly to Death. These meetings follow confrontations, first with Rose and then with Cory, during which Troy manages to kill the love from those he loves the most. In his rage, he tells Death, "I'm gonna build me a fence around what belongs to me. And I want you to stay on the other side. . . . This is between you and me."

The fact that Death is the specter signifies several things. Obviously, Death symbolizes the death of these particular relationships. More importantly, Wilson reminds us that the past is never dead. At the very moments when Troy has failed with his wife and son, Death appears to him, reminding him, and us, that his failed relationship with his father has not died but continues to haunt. Rather than trying to put a fence between his present and his past, Troy needs to construct a bridge. Without making this attempt, Troy will continue to repeat the mistakes of the past he desperately tries to escape.

Cory's relationship with Troy supports this contention. Like Troy, Cory resolves his self-identification by leaving home and the threat to his concept of self. The intergenerational conflict seems to continue with the same unhappy results.

When Cory returns home after Troy's death, he tells his mother that he cannot go to the funeral because "I can't drag Papa with me everywhere I go. I've got to say no to him." Like his father, Cory believes that denying his father is the "way to get rid of that shadow." When Cory finally decides to go to the funeral, he does so because he has come to accept his father's faults and looked to the man himself. Singing the song of Blue, the same song that Troy sang, Cory demonstrates that he can embrace the song of his father without becoming his father. Because he has recognized that he can only be his own man by first acknowledging the foundation laid down by his father for him to build on, Cory, unlike his father, will not be haunted by the past. Continuing to sing the song about his father's dog ties him to his father and to those who came before.

—Pamela Jean Monaco, "Father, Son, and Holy Ghost: From the Local to the Mythical in August Wilson," *August Wilson: A Casebook*, ed. Marilyn Elkins (New York and London: Garland, 1994): pp. 89–104.

John Timpane on Pre- and Post-War Athletics

[John Timpane, coauthor of *Writing Worth Reading*, teaches English at Lafayette College. In this excerpt, Timpane demonstrates how Wilson's play reflects the changing role of the black ballplayer in the 1950s.]

In *Fences*, baseball operates metonymically, as a metaphoric stand-in for the troubled changes of 1957. Much of the action takes place just before the Milwaukee Braves' victory over the New York Yankees in the 1957 World Series. That victory signified a year of many changes in baseball, changes that reflected the social upheavals of 1957. One change, very much in progress, was the emergence of the black ballplayer. Black players had played prominent roles in previous World Series—Willie Mays in the 1964 series and Jackie Robinson in the Brooklyn Dodgers' victory over the Yankees in 1955. Milwaukee was the first non–New York team led by a black star to win a World Series. Hank Aaron, the most powerful hitter in baseball history, played alongside Eddie Mathews, white and a great slugger, and alongside three excellent white pitchers: Warren Spahn, Bob Buhl, and Lew Burdette. Because of the quick rise to prominence of Mays, Aaron, Roberto Clemente, and Frank Robinson, the question was no longer whether blacks would play but whether they could become leaders. As the success of the Braves portended, the answer was yes: Aaron led the league in power statistics, hit a home run on the last day of the season to give the Braves the pennant, rampaged through Yankee pitching to give his team the World Series, and won the National League Most Valuable Player Award for 1957.

Yet the Braves were far from being a truly integrated team, and integration was far from complete in baseball. Though blacks had been playing in the major leagues since 1947, it would take until 1959 for each major league team to have at least one black player. Behind the grudging, piecemeal process of integration in sports lies a Foucaultian "disjunction"—World War II—and a resultant "redistribution": the postwar move west. Hard times in postwar Boston meant dwindling patronage for the Boston Braves, so the team moved west to Milwaukee in 1953, the Dodgers left Brooklyn for Los Angeles, and the New York Giants left for San Francisco. In so doing, these teams mirrored an accelerating westward shift in the center of population. Further, the war probably created new social potential (to this day not completely realized) for women and blacks. For baseball, all this meant new teams, new audiences, and new pressures to tap at last the large pool of talented black players. The National League led in this regard. Indeed, it was not until Frank Robinson was traded from the Cincinnati Reds to the Baltimore Orioles and won the Triple Crown in 1966 that a black player dominated American League pitching the way Mays, Clemente, and Aaron had done in the National League.

Changes in baseball and changes in American life complicate the ability of anyone who, like Troy, bases his assumptions about reality on the facts of a prewar world.

—John Timpane, "Filling the Time: Reading History in the Drama of August Wilson," *May All Your Fences Have Gates: Essays on the Drama of August Wilson*, ed. Alan Nadel (Iowa City: University of Iowa Press, 1994): pp. 67–85.

SANDRA G. SHANNON ON RACE RELATIONS IN THE 1950s

[Sandra G. Shannon, Professor of English at Howard University, is the author of *The Dramatic Vision of August Wilson* and numerous scholarly articles on both Wilson and Amiri Baraka. In this excerpt, Shannon points out how the play captures the tenor of black-white relations in the 1950s.]

While *Ma Rainey's Black Bottom* represents Wilson's idea of the tragedy that results when blacks cannot gain a piece of the American Dream through their music, *Fences* explores similar devastation effected when the sports arena rejects them as well. In *Fences* Wilson fast-forwards past three decades, moving from the pre-Depression era of *Ma Rainey's Black Bottom* to the pre–Civil Rights era to examine the trials of black family life in racist America. World War II has left indelible scars on the Maxson family, just as racial segregation along with unchecked housing and job discrimination forces them to settle for far less than the American Dream promised to the country's veterans, its laborers, and to its citizens—black and white.

The late 1950s were also charged with the electricity of social change. As in Lorraine Hansberry's *Raisin in the Sun* (1959; set sometime after World War II) and Phillip Hayes Dean's *Sty of the Blind Pig* (1973; set in the period just before the beginning of the Civil Rights movement), the characters are in for profound changes in civil rights legislation, race relations, and overall improved conditions for blacks. Still ahead in the 1960s, thousands would march on Washington to demand fair treatment for blacks under the law, Malcolm X and the Reverend Martin Luther King, Jr. would raise the consciousness of the black masses, and discrimination within areas of housing, education, and employment would be significantly eased.

But the 1950s was a decade that brought significant legal action concerning black-white relations. Although in 1953, a federal district court in Washington, D.C., ruled that the doctrine of "separate but equal" permitted federally aided housing projects to bar Negroes if equal housing facilities were available, that doctrine was unanimously overturned by the Supreme Court in the landmark 1954 decision, *Brown v. Board of Education*. In 1955 the Reverend Martin Luther King, Jr. led Montgomery, Alabama, blacks in a boycott of the city's segregated buses, and in 1959 lunch counter segregation was challenged. In this atmosphere of impending positive changes in the country's racial attitudes, several headline sports stories reflected the continued resistance of white America to accepting racial integration: on October 27, 1954, for example, a Texas Court of Appeals in Austin overturned a state law against interracial boxing while on

October 15, 1956, racial segregation of all sports in Louisiana (both for players and spectators) became legally enforceable under a new state law. Undoubtedly, they years extending from the end of World War II to the eve of the Civil Rights movement witnessed mounting racial tensions. August Wilson manages to capture some of this tension in *Fences*.

—Sandra G. Shannon, *The Dramatic Vision of August Wilson* (Washington, D.C.: Howard University Press, 1995): pp. 93–95.

PETER WOLFE ON THE STRENGTH OF TROY

[Peter Wolfe, Professor of English at the University of Missouri, St. Louis, is the author of *Alarms and Epitaphs: The Art of Eric Ambler* and *August Wilson* (Twayne's United States Authors Series). In this excerpt, Wolfe discusses Troy's literal and figurative largesse.]

It's easy to see why Cory kept caving in to Troy during Troy's lifetime. Besides invoking his physical bulk, Troy Maxson's last name calls forth his mighty imagination, a quality reflected by his bursts of eloquence. Troy sprung from his larger-than-life self-image. Rejoicing, suffering, and betraying his intimates on a scale beyond those intimates' imagining, this paragon of vigor dominates whatever environment he occupies because of the raw, demanding surge of his personality.

This power asserts itself straightaway. The play's first scene reveals that he has put his job at risk. Invoking a metaphor from Ralph Ellison's *Invisible Man*, Wilson has placed him "on the carpet." Because he has roiled his coworkers by challenging company policy, he has to report to the commissioner's office. This defier of limits and boundaries recently protested through his union his chiefs' policy of using blacks to lift the heavy garbage cans while leaving the easier work of driving the trucks to the white employees. Troy's brush with authority leaves him unscathed. In fact, Wilson's invocation of Ellison's carpet metaphor soon proves itself to be a red herring. Wilson roused worries in the reader that he planned to dispel and even reverse. Protesting company policy, rather than hurting Troy, helps him. Despite being illiterate and thus unlicensed to drive, he becomes his firm's first black driver.

He achieves this breakthrough by acting in keeping with the grandeur associated with his first name. More of an ancient Greek than a modern Negro, he behaves like a classical hero badgered by the Furies, by fate, and by tragic irony. His pride has stopped him from being wiser or kinder than the rest of us. But it has also leagued with his anger, his inner strength, and his thwarted sense of justice to make him much bolder than we. As his protest to his union shows, he undertakes actions that would daunt and dismay all of the play's other characters. This boldness gives him a stature that invites comparisons with Shakespeare's tragic heroes. The poetic streak that infuses his rage evokes Othello; the Lear-like voracity with which he arrogates life's prizes to himself rests partly on his dearth (or slenderness) of self-knowledge; his arrogance has seduced him into a Coriolanus-like contempt for others. Such qualities remind us that tragic heroes can be brutes, as Hamlet's abuse of Ophelia also shows.

—Peter Wolfe, *August Wilson,* Twayne's United States Authors Series, ed. Frank Day (New York: Twayne Publishers, 1999): pp. 58–59.

JOSEPH H. WESSLING ON THE PLAY AS METACOMEDY

[Joseph H. Wessling is Associate Director of the Ignatian Program and a former Professor of English at Xavier University. In this excerpt, Wessling argues that the play can be considered a comedy of sorts.]

It is easy to make the case that August Wilson's play *Fences* is a tragedy and that Troy Maxson is its tragic protagonist. Few comedies end with a funeral, and there is no denying that Troy's character and life are the stuff of tragedy. But Wilson's vision is much larger than Troy's heroic side, his deeds and omissions. Troy, for all his strengths, is flawed humanity in need of grace and forgiveness.

Such grace and forgiveness are the spirit of true comedy, and a case can be made for viewing *Fences* as a comedy or, perhaps, a metacomedy. The term is taken from Christopher Isherwood, who took it from Gerald Heard: "I think the full horror of life must be depicted, but in the end there should be a comedy which is beyond both comedy and tragedy. The thing Gerald Heard calls 'meta-comedy.'"

Metacomedy, then, is a vision that transcends the immediately comic or tragic. It is not evasive and it has room for pain, for heartache, for alienation, even for death, because it affirms the values of mercy, forgiveness, and sacrifice, which adversity calls forth. For a religious person, metacomedy is what Christopher Fry called a "narrow escape into faith" and a belief in "a universal cause for delight." Fry's metaphor for life is a book of alternating pages of tragedy and comedy. As we read (that is, live) the book, we are anxious about what the last page will be. The comic vision holds that on the last page all will be resolved in laughter. The essence, therefore, of metacomedy is hope, and *Fences* is a lesson in hope.

First there is hope for a better future for African Americans and by extension, for all humankind. If we view Troy's earthly life as an autonomous whole, we are looking at an ultimately tragic book of life. But if we view Troy's life as a page in an ongoing saga, perhaps we can see it not only as a prelude to a happier time but as a success story of itself. George Meredith advises us that to love comedy we must know human beings well enough "not to expect too much of them though you may still hope for good." What should a realist expect of Troy Maxson, who was abandoned by his mother at age eight, fled a brutal, lustful father at age fourteen, began to steal for a living, and served fifteen years on a murder charge? One can only hope for some measure of good, and Troy exceeds a realist's expectations. He holds a steady but disagreeable job as a garbage collector, supports a wife and son, stays sober six days a week, wins his own private civil-rights battle to become a driver, and remains faithful to Rose for eighteen years before he falls.

—Joseph H. Wessling, "Wilson's *Fences*," *Explicator* 57, no. 2 (Winter 1999): pp. 123–7.

[Anna S. Blumenthal is an Associate Professor in the
English and Linguistics Department at Morehouse College.
In this excerpt, Blumenthal suggests that Troy's stories,
while ambiguous, may be viewed as instructive to his son.]

From one perspective, the story of Troy's "devilish" sharecropper
father, who worked his farm relentlessly but who was always in debt
to an unscrupulous white landlord and who took out his frustra-
tions on his children, becomes an opportunity to teach "duty." Troy
notes that his father was not generous, but he tells Lyons that he
approves of his father's "responsibility." Similarly, in the story of his
early life in Mobile, he points out to Lyons that he should not have
had a family before he had the means to support them: "What I do
that for?" Because Rose, the most narrowly moral and the most critical of his listeners, is not even present during these stories, it may be
concluded that using stories to teach male responsibility to his son is
an impulse Wilson shows as coming from Troy himself. His stories
are, in part, consistent with his preachings outside of his narratives,
and the duty-related lessons of his stories are not, it is clear, present
merely to satisfy Rose, who is not among his listeners on this occa-
sion at all. By teaching family responsibility to his son through
stories, he enacts that responsibility which he teaches.

But the two stories he tells here, (two are told perhaps because
Lyons is so impressed and attentive a listener), can also be read as
presenting the cynical case against dutiful devotion to family. The
cynical perspective is more fully developed here than in either of the
earlier stories, despite the fact that Troy's commentary on the stories
helps to narrow he angle between the possible readings by inter-
preting for Lyons the failed examples of duty in the stories as lessons
to be learned from. When Troy's father beats Troy in order to take
his young girlfriend away from his son for his own use, the young
Troy is shocked to discover his father's competitive feelings toward
his own son. Economic deprivation is seen by Wilson, speaking
through Troy, as the trigger for impulses which destroy the bonds
between family members, and this occurs despite a man's will to
work hard and be responsible for his family. A similar pattern
appears in the second story, in which Troy, who can find no work,

must steal to support his young family in Mobile. Stealing, however, lands him in prison, and consequently, Lyons's mother leaves, taking Lyons who must grow up fatherless until he encounters Troy again as an adult. In these stories, the desire to carry out one's "duty" may be interpreted paradoxically, as the root cause for the breakdown of family relationships, which were ironically the reason for undertaking the obligation in the first place.

—Anna S. Blumenthal, "'More Stories Than the Devil Got Sinners': Troy's Stories in August Wilson's *Fences*," *American Drama* 9, no. 2 (Spring 2000): pp. 74–96.

Plot Summary of
Joe Turner's Come and Gone

The supernatural and spiritual elements of *Joe Turner's Come and Gone* have led many critics to speculate that the play rewrites the Christian conversion narrative to incorporate traditional African notions of salvation and sacredness. Set in 1911 in Pittsburgh, when the children of freed African slaves were making their way to cities in search of survival and an identity, this play portrays the difficulties faced by newly uprooted blacks who struggled to reconcile the folk heritage of their African parents with white northern culture. Herald Loomis, who accesses ancient African wisdom and is resurrected from the pain of slavery, is used by Wilson to embody the suffering of, and recuperation from, both slavery and the Great Migration.

As **Act One** opens, Seth Holly, owner of a boarding house and a skilled craftsman, looks out the window as his tenant Bynum performs voodoo. This is the first of many references to African folklore, which attains an elusive status in this play; it is both "mumbo jumbo" and a strong current of spiritual power. Guests and residents begin to people Bertha's kitchen looking for breakfast. Bynum, a conjure man, bases his life on a vision he had on the road one day which showed him the "secret of life" and left him with the power to "bind" people back together who have left one another. His power became possible only because he found out that he had a song, the Binding Song, and that by singing it he could realize his full potential. Rutherford Selig, a white man known as the People Finder, offers to track people down for a fee; as a traveling peddler, he makes extensive contact with people and keeps a running list of customers' whereabouts. Bynum has engaged Selig to find his "Shiny Man," the person whose face shines like new money. Because of his vision, Bynum believes that when he finds this Shiny Man he will know his song has been accepted and has worked its power.

Jeremy, a 25-year-old guitar player, is described by Seth as the backward country type who has not yet realized that the freedom he seeks in the North is not available to blacks. He returns from a night in jail due to an arbitrary arrest by white policemen. Two new guests, a 32 year-old Herald Loomis and his 11 year-old daughter Zonia, arrive looking for a place to stay. They are searching for Loomis' wife

Martha, and at Bynum's suggestion, Loomis decides to ask Rutherford Selig for help. Seth later tells Bertha he has a bad feeling about Loomis and believes the little girl looks just like a local churchgoer named Martha Pentecost. Mattie Campbell, seeking out Bynum's binding powers, asks him to make her estranged husband come back to her. Bynum, who cannot bind what does not cling, tells her to let him go and resume her life. Jeremy offers to be her man until her husband comes back, and after some protestation she obliges.

In the yard, Zonia meets Reuben, the neighbor boy who keeps pigeons that used to belong to his late friend Eugene. Against his grandfather's warnings, Reuben has disobeyed the dying Eugene's request to set his pigeons free and continues to sell the pigeons to Bynum as Eugene himself did. Zonia confides that the only thing she knows about her mother is that someone named Joe Turner did something bad to drive her away.

Scene Two takes place on the following Saturday, again in the kitchen. Seth continues to be suspicious about Loomis and decides he will never reveal the whereabouts of Martha for fear of exposing her to danger. Rutherford Selig agrees, however, to help Loomis for a dollar. Selig boasts that he comes from a long line of People Finders; his grandfather brought slaves to America, and his father found runaway slaves for plantation owners. Now that blacks are no longer slaves, they need help finding each other, which is where Selig has found his niche.

The next morning, in **Scene Three**, Mattie Campbell has decided to move in with Jeremy upstairs. Bynum warns Jeremy not to underestimate the power of a woman, and when Molly Cunningham, a new boarder arrives, Jeremy immediately takes Bynum's words to heart.

In **Scene Four**, which takes place after dinner that evening, it is time to "Juba," as is customary in Seth's household every Sunday. Led by Bynum, all the residents except Loomis participate in an African call and response dance which, as stage directions tell us, is "reminiscent of the ring shouts of the African slaves." In the middle of this frenzied dance, Loomis interrupts in a rage, shouting for all to stop. He unzips his pants, speaks in tongues, and dances around the kitchen. With the help of Bynum, he proceeds to describe a vision he is having in which bones walk on water, sink down, and wash up on the shore as a mass of black-skinned bodies. At the end of his episode, he claims that he is unable to stand up; despite the encouragement of Bynum, he collapses.

Act Two, Scene One begins the next morning with breakfast in Bertha's kitchen, where varied conversations mark the migratory patterns of residents. Seth vows to Bertha that he will not let Loomis stay. Bynum distinguishes between his late father's song (a healing one) and his own song (a binding one). Sharing what she has learned the hard way, Molly tells Mattie that the harder you cling to a man the easier it is for another woman to pull him away. Jeremy, just fired from his job, comes in to find Molly alone and invites her to travel with him. Molly agrees provided he promises not to make her work or travel to the South.

In **Scene Two,** on the following Monday, Loomis is shocked and angered when he hears Bynum singing a song called "Joe Turner's Come and Gone," about a man who after the abolition of slavery captured blacks and kept them as slaves. Bynum can tell that Loomis is one of Joe Turner's slaves because Loomis has forgotten how to sing his song, a song that can only come from deep inside him. Loomis relates that Joe Turner caught him in 1901, just after his daughter was born, and made him a slave for seven years. When he was released, his wife had moved on and left their child with her mother. Ever since then, Loomis and his daughter have been searching for her. Bynum explains that Joe Turner tried to take away Loomis' song, forcing Loomis to bury it and not even know it is inside him. The theme of the lost song becomes a crucial theme in this play. Critics have often suggested that the song represents the identity of an African people that has been forgotten or stifled by slavery.

The **next scene** takes place on Tuesday, the next morning. Jeremy has run off with Molly, and Bertha consoles Mattie by telling her Jeremy was not good enough for her anyway. Loomis attempts to seduce Mattie but finds he cannot touch her. To his dismay, he has forgotten how to touch.

Zonia and Reuben talk in the yard again (**Scene Four**). Reuben says he has seen the ghost of Miss Mabel, Seth's mother. He believes that the late Eugene sent Miss Mabel to scold him for not setting his pigeons free. Both speculate about what would happen if other deceased loved ones returned, revealing their naive but powerfully insightful views of life after death. Reuben, who believes Zonia is the girl he will grow up and marry, kisses her and tells her to wait for him.

When Saturday arrives (**Scene Five**) Loomis and Zonia prepare to leave the boarding house and continue their search for Martha. After their departure, Martha Pentecost arrives looking for them; Rutherford Selig has located her. Her husband and daughter return, and during this animated reunion, Martha explains to an angry and hurt Loomis that leaving Zonia with her mother was the only means of protecting the child's safety. At one point she thought her husband was dead, but since she found out he was alive with her daughter, she has been searching for them. Loomis meanwhile, has been waiting to see her so he can bid her goodbye and "make his own world." He hands his daughter over to her mother.

The climax of this scene occurs when Loomis' anguish over his past overflows. He pulls out a knife and draws blood from his chest in a defiant act against Martha's talk of salvation through the blood of Jesus. He spreads the blood on his face and comes to a realization that for the first time, he can stand up. He has been reborn. Bynum sees Loomis' bloody face and declares that he has found his Shiny Man at last. ✸

List of Characters in
Joe Turner's Come and Gone

Seth Holly is the owner of the boarding house and a skilled craftsman. He dreams of quitting his all-night job and starting his own business manufacturing pots and pans. Both Bynum's voodoo practices and Loomis' deranged demeanor challenge his staid values and creatively upset the equilibrium of his worldview and his home. Being born of Northern free parents, Seth is the only character who has not been uprooted. As such, his stability is important to the others.

Bertha Holly is Seth's wife of 25 years. Her tolerance and charitable attitude offset her husband's often inhospitable suspiciousness and irritability. Her home-cooked meals draw the characters to the kitchen table, where they weave their lives and stories together.

Bynum Walker is known as a conjure man, a rootworker, and a Binder of what Clings. The adversities of life do not ruffle him; he believes in a grand design that makes all circumstances harmonious. He is known to practice voodoo with the blood of pigeons that he buys from Reuben. His entire identity is bound to the conviction that he has found his true song deep inside himself, and with the otherworldly power of this song he can bind people together who have lost each other. He has been searching for a "Shiny Man" who will vindicate his song; that man turns out to be Herald Loomis.

Rutherford Selig, a white man, is a traveling peddler of wares whose extensive customer base allows him to document the whereabouts of people in the region. Known as the great People Finder, he locates Martha Pentecost for Loomis, her estranged husband.

Herald Loomis, visitor to the boarding house, is a severely troubled ex-slave of Joe Turner, a man who kidnapped blacks to bind them as slaves illegally after abolition. Since his release by Turner, Loomis and his daughter have been searching for Martha, his wife. When he reunites with her, Loomis feels he can finally say the goodbye that will grant him the freedom to recreate his life. As a result of two visions, one representing his terror and the other his salvation, Loomis for the first time in his life finds he has a place in the world and two legs on which to stand.

Zonia Loomis is Herald's 11 year-old daughter. Shortly after her birth, Herald was captured by Turner and kept as a slave for seven years. During this time, Martha handed Zonia over to Martha's mother until Herald returned, after which the two set out looking for Martha. When they find Martha, Herald turns Zonia over to her. Zonia's despair over being emotionally relocated yet again is poignantly clear as she pleads with her departing father.

Mattie Campbell has suffered the loss of two children who died in infancy and a husband who left her because he thought she was cursed. She appeals to Bynum to bring her husband back to her again, but instead she receives his advice on how to grieve his loss and continue her life without him. By the end of the play, her attention is drawn to Herald Loomis, who has also been healed. She pursues him as runs out of the house and into his future.

Reuben Mercer is a young boy who lives with his grandfather next door to the Holly's. He keeps and sells pigeons that once belonged to his deceased friend Eugene, despite the latter's dying request that he set the pigeons free. Reuben is haunted one night by the ghost of Miss Mabel, Seth's late mother, who scolds Reuben for not freeing the pigeons. Reuben befriends Zonia and insists that she is the girl he is supposed to marry when he grows up.

Molly Cunningham is a very attractive young woman who has landed at the Holly's supposedly because she missed her train. As a result of being abandoned by her man, she has detached herself from love and made a life as, in Bertha's words, "that kind of woman run off with the first man got a dollar to spend on her" (II.iii). Her philosophy of life is: "I don't trust nobody but the good Lord above, and I don't love nobody but my mama" (II.i). To Mattie's disappointment, Molly leaves town with Jeremy.

Martha Pentecost, formerly Martha Loomis, is Herald Loomis' estranged wife. Having lost Herald to Joe Turner, she found her way in the world through Christianity. Led back to Herald by Rutherford Selig, she gets a chance to see and take custody of her child after many years. Martha tries to persuade Herald to repent as a Christian, sending him into a defiant rage that leads eventually to a uniquely personal resurrection for him.

Joe Turner, whom the audience only hears about, is based on the actual Joe Turner of Memphis, Tennessee who captured and enslaved black men after the abolition of slavery. The women of Memphis sing a song called "Joe Turner's Come and Gone," which means he has captured their men. According to Bynum, Joe Turner continued to incarcerate new slaves every seven years because he was desperately seeking to steal someone's song. Herald Loomis was one of Joe Turner's slaves.

Jeremy Furlow, an eager and restless young man whose affections waver between the hard-working Mattie Campbell and the indolent, seductive Molly Cunningham. ❀

Critical Views on
Joe Turner's Come and Gone

PATRICIA GANTT ON SOUTHERN PERSONALITIES
IN THE PLAY

[Patricia Gantt teaches English at Utah State University and
chairs the English Education Committee. Her published
articles include topics such as teaching the Holocaust and
Faulkner's fiction. In this excerpt, Gantt argues that despite
the play's northern setting, its Southern characters carry
within them the pain of the South.]

The first play in the historic cycle is *Joe Turner's Come and Gone,* a
drama full of the sounds and memories of the South. Because the
majority of the characters were born in the South or are only a
generation away from it, it is no surprise that the texture of
southern life is evident in much they say and do. Pittsburgh city
people now, they still use a language laden with rural vernacular: a
man is "hungrier than a mule"; a child who will not eat is "skinny
as a bean pole"; a person on the edge of an action is "fixing to" do
it; things beneath consideration are those a person "ain't studying."
Characters' speech is often rich with folk lyrics, as when a man
recalls John Henry's "ten-pound hammer" in bragging about his
own sexual prowess. Folk belief and folk wisdom, too, are part of
the play. One of the chief characters is Bynum, a conjure man
skilled in the old ways of roots and potions. Consulted by a woman
grieving for her missing man, Bynum gives her a packet to put
under her pillow to "bring good luck to you. Draw it to you like a
magnet." Southern foodways, too, have made the northern journey,
as folks gathered around the table share grits, yams, biscuits, or
fried chicken. Out of the physical south themselves, *Joe Turner's*
people carry much of the South within.

The principal southern legacy they share, however, is their
memory of the slave past, which Wilson brings into the play from its
inception. The prologue places the action in the context of the dias-
pora—especially southern slavery—with a lyrical description of the
migration of the "sons and daughters of newly freed African slaves"
to the great cities of the north, where they hope to shape "a new

identity as free men of definite and sincere worth." "Foreigners in a strange land . . . Isolated, cut off from memory . . . they arrive dazed and stunned" by all they have endured, mostly in the rural South. The psychological baggage they carry is considerable: refused full access both to their African heritage and to modern financial and political power, they desire ways to "give clear and luminous meaning" to the as-yet unarticulated song they carry within, one composed of both "a wail and a whelp of joy." They arrive "carrying Bibles and guitars," symbols of old faith and new songs. In this play, as in others, Wilson is not reluctant to explore the slave past, about which he says: "Blacks in America want to forget about slavery—the stigma, the shame. That's the wrong move. If you can't be who you are, who can you be? How can you know what to do?" For *Joe Turner*'s characters, the quest for identity and the pain of slavery's memories are inextricably bound.

—Patricia Gantt, "Ghosts from 'Down There': The Southernness of August Wilson," *August Wilson: A Casebook,* ed. Marilyn Elkins (New York and London: Garland, 1994): pp. 69–88.

MISSY DEHN KUBITSCHEK ON BERTHA'S AND BYNUM'S SHAMANISM

[Missy Dehn Kubitschek is a Professor of English, Afro-American Studies, and Women's Studies at Indiana University-Purdue University at Indianapolis. She is the author of *Claiming the Heritage: African-American Women Novelists and History.* In this excerpt, Kubitschek discusses gender roles as they relate to spiritual healing.]

Joe Turner presents two African American spiritual workers, Bertha and Bynum, who labor to ensure healthy continuity in their community. In general, same-gender advice seems to be better understood than trans-gender talk; that is, Bertha works well with Mattie, and Bynum with Loomis, to develop or restore individuals to a state in which they can maintain stable sexual and emotional relationships. When Bynum tries to persuade Mattie not to pursue the husband who abandoned her, he discourses on the dangers in using spiritual forces to bind artificially rather than reinforcing what clings of its own nature. His language is metaphorical, visionary, abstract:

> And if he ain't supposed to come back . . . then he'll be in your bed one morning and it'll come up on him that he's in the wrong place. Then he's lost outside of time from his place that he's supposed to be in. Then both of you be lost and trapped outside of life and ain't no way for you to get back in it.

When Bertha consoles Mattie, on the other hand, she uses concrete speech:

> Jeremy ain't had enough to him. You need a man who's got some understanding and who willing to work with that understanding to come to the best he can. You got your time coming. You just tries too hard. . . . You get all that trouble off your mind and just when it look like you ain't never gonna find what you want . . . you look up it's standing right there. That's how I met my Seth.

Further, Bertha offers Mattie her own experience as a hopeful model. Both men and women seem most effective in counseling others of their own sex, then, and their languages differ almost as much as those of Troy and Rose in *Fences*.

Joe Turner concentrates on male-to-male spiritual communications, as Loomis becomes One Who Goes Before and Shows the Way in his turn; Bertha's spirituality appears explicitly in the stage directions, as Gabriel's does in *Fences*. Significantly, however, male and female shamans in *Joe Turner* share rituals and ritual space; African American spirituality does not assume or enforce separate, unequal spheres. First, women are not shut out of economic power—Bertha's kitchen is a source of revenue (through its importance to the boardinghouse). Second, whereas in *Fences* the location of Rose's spiritual power is offstage, in her church, in *Joe Turner* the kitchen is a ritual ground in which both Bertha and Bynum function. Here Bertha exorcises melancholy and refreshes the community through contagious laughter; here Bynum's call and response guides not only Loomis's understanding of his vision but the community's juba. Both shamans heal, and they address individuals or community according to need. Third, Bynum provides the clearest example of the divergence of African American and European understandings of men's and women's powers; his role would be unthinkable for a European male because it requires giving of oneself to bind others— the specifically female role of the separate-spheres paradigm.

—Missy Dehn Kubitschek, "August Wilson's Gender Lesson," *May All Your Fences Have Gates,* ed. Alan Nadel (Iowa City: University of Iowa Press, 1994): pp. 182–199.

TRUDIER HARRIS ON AFRICANIZING THE AUDIENCE

[Trudier Harris is a J. Carlyle Sitterston Professor of English at the University of North Carolina at Chapel Hill and the author of *From Mammies to Militants: Domestics in Black American Literature, Black Women in the Fiction of James Baldwin, Fiction and Folklore: The Novels of Toni Morrison,* and *The Power of the Porch: The Storyteller's Craft in Zora Neale Hurston, Gloria Naylor, and Randall Kenan.* In this excerpt, Harris suggests that Wilson uses Bynum's story to transport white viewers, represented by Selig, into a black reality.]

Wilson alters, slightly but perceptively, our expectations of African American tradition by similarly redefining the audiences toward whom tellers direct their narratives. Storytelling occurs at significant points in the play, one of which is shortly after Bynum performs his initial ceremony with the pigeons. He relates the tale of "the shiny man," that spiritual, otherworldly being who has determined his path as a conjure man. Although we have been introduced to Seth and Bertha, they are not the primary audience to whom Bynum directs his story; indeed, Seth is offstage at that point. He selects Selig, the white peddler/"People Finder" instead; he has earlier sent Selig in search of "the shiny man."

This choice is an intriguing one, for it we were to adhere to stereo-type, we might assume that the white Selig would be less inclined to respond favorably to Bynum's tale of having encountered a shiny man and that Seth, a black man, and Bertha, a black woman, would be more receptive. So the question immediately arises as to why

Wilson would have made this choice. Obviously there is the functional reason of conveying information to the viewing audience. That information immerses them in a worldview that equates knowing the self with the meaning of life and that equates the meaning of life with an individual song that in turn defines the self. This circular interrelatedness of one human being to another links Bynum to "the shiny man" for whom he has hired Selig to search, and it further links the audience to the action onstage. The story of Bynum's encounter with "the shiny man" therefore begins the process of "Africanizing the audience" that is inherent in Wilson's presenting the lore as a given rather than arguing for its acceptance. I use the phrase "Africanizing the audience" to encompass the white viewers who undoubtedly made up the majority of the viewing audience for Wilson's play; of course African Americans in the audience would simply have their beliefs reinforced, or—in the case of those upwardly mobile (like Seth) who have forgotten their roots—reclaimed. The immediate audience (Selig) and the viewing audience are thus simultaneously encouraged to a different way of perceiving reality, to understand that it is possible to see around corners, as the Invisible Man would say. Selig's skepticism might mirror that of those viewing the play, but neither can erase from memory Bynum's tale of "the shiny man." Wilson thereby gives whites no choice but to become immersed in a black reality.

—Trudier Harris, "August Wilson's Folk Traditions," *August Wilson: A Casebook,* ed. Marylin Elkins (New York and London: Garland Publishing, 1994): pp. 49–67.

DOUGLAS ANDERSON ON AFRO-BAPTIST AND BIBLICAL SOURCES FOR BYNUM'S CONVERSION NARRATIVE

[In this excerpt, Douglas Anderson points out the rich and varied spiritual traditions embodied in Bynum's conversion narrative.]

Bynum's narrative of revelation and self-recovery resembles Afro-Baptist conversion narratives. In these narratives, according to

Michael Sobel, a "seeker" makes a journey that leads him not only to rebirth in Christ but to recovery of his essential self, "the 'little me' in the 'big me.'" Though unique, this self is also a manifestation of a collective spirit that, Sobel suggests, "the Black had brought . . . with him from Africa, not as a deity but in his own inner self." By recovering the 'little me,' the convert is both reborn in Christ and "brought . . . back to his African heritage." As in Afro-Baptist conversion, the self recovered by Bynum was both unique (his personal "song") and already there and waiting for him as part of his African heritage, a self related to an ancestral or ethnic past. Thus, the place where Bynum was taught "the Secret of Life" and learned how to find his song was one that lay on a road Bynum had already traveled, and he received instruction from an ancestor, the spirit of his father. As "the One Who Goes Before and Shows the Way," the shiny man was potentially both spiritual guide and spiritual ancestor.

Elements of Bynum's narrative of revelation and self-recovery evoke the Biblical story of Saul's transformative encounter with a risen Christ on the road to Damascus. Reading Bynum's story through the Biblical one suggests that the shiny man who guided Bynum toward his song and then disappeared in blinding light was a Christ figure from whom Bynum received a new identity, just as Saul, the persecutor of Christians, was transformed into Paul, the great preacher of the gospel. Bynum himself, according to this paradigm, would be a reborn Paul and his "binding song" the task of uniting African Americans in anticipation of a returning savior or messiah. Bynum does, in fact, hope to see the shiny man again, but the person and the advent he waits for do not have quite the meaning that they have in the Biblical paradigm. If the shiny man is a messiah figure, he is not an otherworldly or even exceptional individual. As Bynum tells Selig, "I ain't even so sure he's one special fellow. That shine could pass on to anybody. He could be anybody shining." The shiny man is an ordinary man who, possessing his song as "a voice inside him telling him which way to go," is able to guide others toward repossession of their songs, toward becoming shiny men in their own right. And since "that shine could pass on to anybody," the shiny man is also the individual who has not yet found his song, one who searches for himself. That search takes place in the world, and for Bynum to see the shiny man "again" means assisting that search by acting as the shiny-man guide to another. Seeing the shiny man again does not entail Bynum's deliverance from the world but confirmation of his contribution to it. As Bynum's father told him, "There was lots of shiny men and if I ever saw one again before I died then I would know that my song had been accepted and worked its full power in the world. . . ."

—Douglas Anderson, "Saying Goodbye to the Past: Self-Empowerment and History," *CLA Journal* 40, no. 4 (June 1997): pp. 432–57.

SANDRA G. SHANNON ON SHINY MAN AS SURROGATE GOD

[Sandra G. Shannon, Professor of English at Howard University, is the author of *The Dramatic Vision of August Wilson* and scholarly articles on both Wilson and Amiri Baraka. In this excerpt, Shannon shows how Shiny Man compensates for the insufficiency of the white man's god.]

To understand how Bynum's quest for Shiny Man fits into Wilson's larger agenda, one must step back from the play as one would from an impressionistic painting. One must first understand that Shiny Man is the African alternative to what August Wilson calls "the white man's God." He explains in an interview,

> Amiri Baraka has said that when you look in the mirror, you should see your God. If you don't, you have somebody else's God. So, in fact, what you do is worship an image of God, which is white, which is the image of the very same people who have oppressed you, who have put you on the slave ships, who have beaten you, and who have forced you to work.

This elusive deity who overwhelms Bynum and leads him to the spirit of his deceased father apparently answered Bynum's own spiritual probings. Shiny Man, therefore, personifies Wilson's alternative to oppressive images that he associates with Christianity.

In the greater scheme of Wilson's decade-by-decade revision of African American history, Bynum is a chief player. This initially misunderstood conjure man is the catalyst for Wilson's historical approach to the troubling record of African American experience in the United States. In *Joe Turner* he is the only character empowered with the ability to forge ties between Africa and America. Only the African healer and rootworker possesses the antidote to the cultural fragmentation that slowly devastates his fellow boardinghouse neighbors. As a conduit between Africa and America (past and present), he conjures up fields of experience whereby African Americans can counter their present cultural alienation by drawing upon the wisdom of their ancestors.

Bynum's quest for Shiny Man parallels Loomis's search for his identity and, by extension, becomes every black man's search for affirmation in a world with few gods and even fewer monuments to his past.

—Sandra G. Shannon, *The Dramatic Vision of August Wilson* (Washington, D.C.: Howard University Press, 1995): pp. 137–138.

MARY L. BOGUMIL ON THE CULTURAL AND ETYMOLOGICAL ORIGINS OF THE JUBA

[Mary L. Bogumil teaches Modern British and American Literature at Southern Illinois University, Carbondale. She is the author of *Understanding August Wilson* and scholarly articles on authors including Harold Pinter, Langston Hughes, and Richard Wright. In this excerpt, Bogumil demonstrates the Juba's power to evoke African ancestry.]

In Wilson's play the juba signifies the recurrence (in memories, in deeds, and in visions) of remote ancestral ties—a paternal, cultural legacy from the characters' African forefathers. Yet as scholarship on this subject indicates, the juba's origins and the interpretations surrounding the motivation for its practice are somewhat difficult to delineate. For example, Beverly J. Robinson analyzes one possible origin of the dance: "One of the earliest records of the term *juba* dates back to American minstrelsy. Both Juba and Jube consistently appeared as names of enslaved Africans who were skilled musicians and dancers. The father of a celebrated black artist who was popular outside the minstrelsy circuit, Horace or Howard Weston, was named Jube." Robinson elaborates upon the myriad etymological origins of the word *juba: juba* or *diuba* in Bantu, which literally translated means "to pat, beat time, the sun, the hour." Linguistically the word *juba* comes from the African *giouba* referring to a sacred polyrhythmic African step dance whose secular origins trace back to South Carolina and the West Indies, where the word referred to both a mixture of leftovers consumed by the plantation slaves and a song that they created to prepare them psychologically to eat what Robinson calls "slop."

If the reader of Wilson's play considers the following explication of the term in the *Oxford English Dictionary,* the cause of Herald Loomis's mental breakdown (or epiphany) and the juba's purgative effect upon him become clear. The *OED* defines *juba,* sometimes spelled "juber" or "jouba," as a species of dance that often included the reenactment of a mental breakdown. It was performed by the antebellum plantation slaves in the Deep South—a dance whose choreography consisted of the clapping of hands, the patting of knees and thighs, the striking of feet on the floor, and the singing of a refrain in which the word *juba* was repeated, a refrain that acted as an incantation to the Holy Ghost or an invocation to manifest a transcendent being.

Certainly, this mode of call-and-response communication was the only vehicle to voice a sense of community—not unlike the call-and-response spirituals that were sung by slaves on one plantation to communicate with those on another nearby plantation—in an environment where a sense of community was systematically undermined by the institution of slavery. In the same way, Bynum Walker as the Afrocentric spiritual healer in the play leads the disillusioned Herald Loomis through a series of questions to recall his African identity.

—Mary L. Bogumil, *Understanding August Wilson* (Columbia: University of South Carolina Press, 1999): pp. 55–57.

Plot Summary of
Two Trains Running

Many of the "significant" events in *Two Trains Running* seem to take place offstage: the spectacle of Prophet Samuel's death, the Malcolm X rally, the miraculous deeds of Aunt Ester, the mysterious death of Hambone, and Memphis' life-changing court appearances. Separated but not far from these events, the action of the play that is visible to the audience occurs in Memphis' dilapidated diner, where commentaries on offstage action construct both the stories and the storytellers. Post–civil rights American history is being made outside Memphis' doors, but the audience experiences this history through the personal conflicts of a few people looking for luck in a small, run-down diner in Pittsburgh.

Act One, Scene One opens in Memphis' diner, the social hub of the neighborhood and the setting of all action in the play. This scene introduces the theme of chance and luckiness, as we learn that each character plays to win against considerable odds. Wolf is a numbers runner who uses Memphis' phone to take bets from hopeful players. Memphis eagerly awaits a call from a lawyer who might help him cash in on the sale of his property to the city. Sterling, just released from the penitentiary and down on his luck, is looking for a job and a woman. Holloway's ticket to happiness lies in the wisdom of Aunt Ester, the local psychic whose powers "make you right with yourself." Hambone, who believes he was undercompensated for painting Mr. Lutz's fence long ago, has uttered the same sentence for nine and a half years in an attempt to get a side of ham. Meanwhile, across the street at West's funeral parlor, people line up to view the body of the late reverend Prophet Samuel and rub his head for good luck.

Memphis reveals in **Scene Two** that he once owned a farm in Jackson and has sworn vengeance on Mr. Stovall, the man responsible for driving him off his land. The only thing preventing Memphis from taking revenge with a 30.06 is the literal and symbolic distance between himself and the depot; there are two trains running every day, and he only needs to get on one of them. Meanwhile Risa, the waitress, wears the self-inflicted scars signifying her own torment. She has slashed her legs with a razor to make them as ugly as possible in order to discourage men from looking at her as a sex object. Wolf prophetically determines that all she needs is one good man. The rally in honor of the late Malcolm X's birthday is scheduled for the same evening, which sparks an animated conversation about the late activist. Memphis' cold logic says there is no such thing as justice and a gun is the only way to get through to the white man. Holloway's spiritualism leads him to compare Malcolm X with martyrs like Saint Paul and Saint Peter, while Sterling admires the man for daring to tell the truth.

In **Scene Three**, Sterling tells the group that he was raised in an orphanage and landed in jail by robbing a bank during a desperate time following the death of his foster father. He is attracted to Risa and invites her to the Malcolm X rally. In an effort to help her out of her extreme self-consciousness, he tells her that people notice her much less than she imagines. Sterling then attempts to break Hambone out of his shell by teaching him to say "Black is beautiful." Memphis meanwhile has fired his black lawyer for backing down to the city, replacing him with a white lawyer and renewing his resolution to get a fair price of $25,000 for his land.

Act Two, Scene One is incendiary in several ways. Sterling ignites a romantic flame with Risa by offering her some stolen flowers and making plans to seek out Aunt Ester's blessing for their marriage. He sells Memphis a can of gasoline near a grill that tends to go up in flames, and he buys a gun from Wolf on credit. Memphis' temper flares as he berates Wolf for tying up his phone line again, then turns his anger toward the white people in Jackson who many years ago killed his mule and set fire to his crops. Shunning West's shady offer to buy his current property, he vows that he will not only get his just price from the city but he will ensure that justice is done in Jackson. As the emotions wind down, the focus shifts to Aunt Ester and her idiosyncratic practices, since Sterling has visited her only to find that she was sleeping. West tells the group that he went to her to find out if his wife was in heaven but dismissed her as crazy when she asked him to pay her by throwing his money into the river. Holloway, however, is convinced that by laying her hands on his head she freed him from the urge to kill his grandfather and ensured that his grandfather died of "natural causes."

When **Scene Two** begins, Holloway announces that Hambone, who in nine and a half years has not missed a single day of pressuring Mr. Lutz about his ham, is nowhere to be found. Prophet

Samuel having been buried at long last, is also gone. The absent Sterling poses a threat as Wolf imagines he will react violently when he finds out that his winning number will only receive half the money due to number cutting. Memphis, a bit lost though unwilling to admit it, asks Holloway for Aunt Ester's address.

Hambone's whereabouts are finally revealed in **Scene Three**: he has died fully clothed on his bed. Risa dreams of buying him a $700 casket, while Sterling dreams of increasing his winnings in Vegas to the tune of three cadillacs. In contrast to these two, West warns: "carry you a little cup through life and you'll never be disappointed." Sterling, as predicted, is angry that his number has been cut and storms off to see Alberts, Wolf's boss. In **Scene Four**, Sterling returns from seeing Alberts, whom he has convinced to return the $2 he put down for the bet. He has also visited Aunt Ester, who assured him that Risa is the woman for him. "I cannot swim does not walk by the lakeside," Ester told Sterling, giving an accurate reading of his inability to stay away from trouble. Though Risa resists Sterling's amorous advances, she is soon kissing him passionately.

In **Scene Five**, conflicts are ignited as quickly as they are resolved. Sterling has viewed Hambone's casket and remarks how peaceful he looks. The Malcolm X rally has come and gone without any violence, but Wolf sarcastically notes that policemen were taking pictures, something they would never do at white people's meetings. A drunken Memphis, who has been offered $35,000 for his property, tells Risa to buy flowers for Hambone in honor of everyone who has ever "dropped the ball and picked it back up." Still unsatisfied, however, he interprets Ester's cryptic advice as a call to return to Jackson and demand his property back from Stovall. Suddenly everyone hears the sound of glass breaking and a burglar alarm: Sterling, with bleeding face and hands, presents a stolen ham as the perfect addition to Hambone's casket. ❀

List of Characters in
Two Trains Running

Memphis is the owner of a diner that will soon be bought by the city and demolished. He wants to return to Jackson to reclaim the farm that was wrongfully taken from him by Mr. Stovall through legal trickery and death threats. In addition, he has lawyers working to get him a good price for his current property. He is nostalgic for time passed, when the neighborhood was thriving and his restaurant was busy. His wife has left him abruptly after 22 years. He mistrusts idealistic abstractions such as "freedom" and "justice," and though he put his gun down years ago, he believes it is the only way for a black man to get white men's attention.

Wolf is the local numbers runner who conducts his business from the telephone booth in Memphis' restaurant. He believes that getting a winning number is the only way his people can get lucky in a world where a black man can be put in jail for no reason at all. Sterling bets a winning number with him, but he can only pay off half the amount, since his boss Alberts cuts the numbers when there are multiple winners.

Risa is the waitress at the restaurant. She is good-natured and protective toward Hambone, but guarded against men who make amorous advances. The ugly scars on her legs mark her attempt to make herself uglier so men will not look at her merely as a sexual object. Though Wolf claims to know her best, it is Sterling who breaks through her rough exterior to release her sexual passion.

Holloway is an older man whose opinions tend to honor the dignity of his fellows. He thinks Hambone has more sense than most people because rather than take on shame, he places shame on Lutz for underpaying him. He claims that blacks, far from lazy, are the hardest workers because they worked for free for 300 years. His champion is Aunt Ester, whom he regards as a great seer with an uncanny understanding; it is she who miraculously freed him from the desire to kill his grandfather.

Sterling is an ex-convict raised in an orphanage whose charm and genuine affection toward others makes up for his tendency to steal and freeload. He manages to bet a winning number, teach Hambone new sentences, win over Risa, acquire a gun, and wreak revenge on Mr. Lutz in a matter of two days. As Aunt Ester tells him "I cannot swim does not walk by the lakeside" and she is correct, since Sterling strides up to trouble without hesitation. Memphis predicts Sterling will be back in jail within three weeks, and Sterling justifies that prediction by stealing a ham from Mr. Lutz's shop and leaving a bloody trail.

Hambone is a neighborhood madman who has been reliving a conflict that happened nine and a half years ago. On this fateful day, Hambone painted Mr. Lutz the butcher's fence and for his work he received a chicken. Because he believes he should have gotten a ham, he has ever since then appeared daily to chant "He gonna give me my ham." Sterling helps him to say "Black is beautiful" and other new phrases, but he dies never having gotten his ham. After his sudden but peaceful death, Sterling steals a ham from Lutz to place in Hambone's coffin.

West is the crooked funeral director whose parlor is across the street from the restaurant. Owner of many properties, he makes his fortune selling overpriced caskets, selling sham leak insurance for coffins, and recycling suits for the dead. He remarks at how the families of the deceased ultimately care only about the valuables left behind. West offers Memphis large cash sums for his plot, hoping to acquire it so that he can sell it to the city for a profit.

Aunt Ester is the local psychic whom some believe is over three hundred years old. Critics compare her age to the duration of slavery. According to Holloway, her uncanny power allows her to wash people's souls and leave them with a profound inner peace. She is the only character who has no use for money, demanding that her visitors pay her by throwing their money in the river. Though we never see her, she constitutes a significant presence in the play as the source of folklore and speculations on otherworldly powers. ❀

Critical Views on
Two Trains Running

LISA WILDE ON CHANCE AND THE OCCULT

[In this excerpt, Lisa Wilde discusses the ways in which gambling and supernatural elements in the play introduce new rules into an otherwise losing game for the black man.]

The insistent rhythm of time and mortality pulses through the play. The restaurant is across the street from Lutz's Meat Market and West's Funeral Home—the characters travel between these three primitive sites of slaughter, consumption and decay. People speculate about the last days of the world. The block the restaurant is on is scheduled to be levelled. West, the undertaker, goes about the ancient rituals of preparing the dead for the afterlife. He is a modern high priest officiating over the ceremonies of grief and valediction. Yet an impulse towards action emerges out of this desolation. Risa, Holloway, Sterling and Memphis try to find their own ways to envisage a future through consulting prophets and oracles, playing with chance. Wolf, the numbers runner, offers new lives and different endings for the price of a ticket.

Playing the numbers is a way to try to control fate and get enough money to get ahead. There is no logic to the world: getting ahead happens only through a lucky number or a sudden contract. Working, particularly working according to standards imposed by white America, yields up only a slight variant on slavery. The real battle is revealed to be one not of language or attitude but of economics. Wilson tells stories of people inadequately recompensed for the work they've done, legal clauses written so a property owner can be bought out for a fraction of the price he paid, even lottery winnings that are cut in half. The only way to recover what has been lost or stolen is by following the dominant culture's tactics: robbery, burning buildings for insurance, carrying guns to assert power. But these people are arrested and imprisoned for actions that in the marketplace would be considered shrewd business. Wilson's characters are not innocent: they have already tried to make their lives work as the world dictates and lost. Their need to reclaim what has been taken from them, either in actual or symbolic terms—Herald Loomis' lost wife in *Joe Turner's Come and Gone*, the piano bought with a father's blood in *The Piano Lesson*, Memphis' farm—becomes the truest form of revolution and affirmation.

In each of Wilson's plays, this liberating moment comes through communicating with the supernatural or occult mysteries. Troy Maxson in *Fences* wrestles with Death and ultimately loses; his brother Gabriel sends him off to the hereafter with a blast of sound and an outpouring of light. *Joe Turner's* Bynum helps Loomis discover his hidden song through a ritual purging. Boy Willie must wrestle with Sutter's ghost as his sister Berneice exorcises the suffering from the piano by touching it in *The Piano Lesson*. In *Two Trains Running*, travelers seeking answers are sent to the red door at 1839 Wylie Street to consult Aunt Ester, a three hundred and twenty-two year old prophetess. Like the Cumaean Sibyl or the Sphinx, she provides her pilgrims not with answers but with riddles and parables, divinations that they themselves must interpret. Specifically, she offers them the choice of remaining passive or moving towards their fate—if they are ready to walk through fire to reach it. She may extend healing but the comfort comes with a knife's edge. Her presence, reaching back to precolonial days, represents African American memory: the choice is to ignore it or to retrieve it. As Memphis says of his own travels, "I'm going back there one day. . . . They've got two trains running every day."

—Lisa Wilde, "Reclaiming the Past: Narrative and Memory in August Wilson's *Two Trains Running*," *Theater* 22, no. 1 (Fall/Winter 1990-1991): pp. 73–4.

KIM MARRA ON RISA AND BLACK FEMALE SELF-HATRED

[Kim Marra teaches Theatre at the University of Iowa and has published numerous articles on gender production in the theatre. In this excerpt, Marra suggests that Risa's self-mutilation both challenges and internalizes sexist and racist ideologies.]

In addition to the narratives of the male characters, Wilson also conveys a powerful ideological message about gender through Risa, the play's only female character. Her most outstanding characteristic, one to which almost every personage in the play refers at least once, is the fact that she has cut herself. Advising Sterling to play the number 781, she divulges that she has 7 scars on one leg and 8 on the other, but she will not say where the 1 is. Her modesty suggests she has mutilated her genitals, a supposition consistent with Memphis's claim that her self-inflicted scars have rendered her "unnatural," that is, "unwomanly."

On one hand, this is a compelling gesture of self-assertion and defiance of stereotypes within which traditional perceptions of black women would confine her. Refusing to be seen chiefly as a degraded sex object, Holloway tells us, "she figure if she made her legs ugly that would force everybody to look at her and see what kind of personality she is." Though male characters' continued phallocentric responses to her indicate the futility of her strategy, she persists in her defiance, challenging Memphis on his claim that he treated his wife "like she was the Queen of Sheba," and taking her time filling his imperious orders. She has also pledged allegiance to Prophet Samuel and, by extension, to the matriarchal deity, Aunt Ester.

On the other had, her self-mutilation also indicates her extreme internalization of the racist, sexist ideology of black female degradation. Her behavior reflects the phenomenon of black female self-hatred described by black feminists, an abhorrence of and desire to destroy the black body which disqualifies her from meeting standards of ideal femininity under white supremacist capitalist patriarchy. In addition to economic necessity, internalized degradation and self-hatred keep her working for the abusive male chauvinist tyrant, Memphis. These forces also compel her to compromise her defiant sense of selfhood by agreeing to go to Vegas with Sterling, a man who represents much of what she had eschewed in the opposite sex.

Significantly, in falling for Sterling, Risa accompanies him to festivities marking the birthday of Malcolm X. Historicizing the play with this plot device, Wilson inscribes both characters within black nationalist gender ideology. Sterling's phallocentric masculine ethos is elevated via worship of the civil rights leader lauded for giving African Americans their "manhood," while Risa is destined to become "man's field to produce his nation." She betrays not only her independence but her matriarchal allegiance to Aunt Ester in honoring a martyred prophet whose faith was rooted in the vehemently patriarchal Islamic teachings of Elijah Muhammed. Through association with Malcolm X, the romantic relationship between Sterling and Risa, rather than healing the gender divisions endemic to Wilson's racial history, indicates victory of the phallocentric black male over the potentially castrating black female.

—Kim Marra, "Ma Rainey and the Boyz: Gender Ideology in August Wilson's Broadway Canon," *August Wilson: A Casebook,* ed. Marylin Elkins (New York and London: Garland Publishing, 1994): pp. 123–160.

Mark William Rocha on Overhearing Holloway

[Mark William Rocha teaches English at California State University, Northridge. In this excerpt, Rocha discusses Holloway's loud voice as compensating for the unheard voices of African Americans throughout history.]

In a staged performance of *Two Trains Running,* Holloway, the community elder and oral historian, most often speaks while seated in his regular booth in Memphis's restaurant. This booth is upstage right and places Holloway closest to the audience, which he faces when speaking. For this character's longest speech about the black man's historical relationship to America's capitalist economy, director Lloyd Richards has blocked the action onstage so that Holloway rises from his booth, walks to the exact middle of the stage, and in Brechtian fashion faces the audience, whom he appears to address directly.

> It's simple mathematics. Ain't no money in niggers working. Look out there on the street. If there was some money in it, if the white man could figure out a way to make some money by putting niggers to work, we'd all be working. He ain't building no more railroads. He got them. He ain't building no more highways. Somebody already stuck the telephone poles in the ground. That's been done already. The white man ain't stacking no more niggers. You know what I'm talking about stacking niggers, don't you?

The blocking of the stage action makes explicit the usually implicit theatrical premise that there are two addressees of Holloway's speeches, the other black characters in Memphis's restaurant and the mostly white audiences of August Wilson's play. This establishes the triadic relationship that is essential to what in the black vernacular is referred to as "loud-talking," one of the ritual performances that Henry Louis Gates classified as an example of signifyin(g). According to Gates:

> One successfully loud-talks by speaking to a second person remarks in fact directed to a third person, at a level just audible to the third person. A sign of the success of this practice is an indignant "What?" from the third person, to which the speaker replies, "I wasn't talking to you." Of course, the speaker was, yet simultaneously was not.

With recourse to Gates and Claudia Mitchell-Kernan, upon whose description of signifyin(g) and loud-talking Gates relies, I want to propose loud-talking as the paradigmatic metaphor for the African American theater in general and for August Wilson's history plays in particular. In the above example from *Two Trains Running*, Holloway—or, one should properly say, the actor playing Holloway—is consciously loud-talking one audience, ostensibly addressing in this case the character of Memphis, played by a fellow black actor, but really intending to elicit a response from a "third person"—the members of the audience—that will establish an audience's relationship to the represented experience onstage. This is the purpose of Holloway's overtly historical question which alludes to the middle passage, "You know what I'm talking about stacking niggers, don't you?" One's response to this question largely determines the historical "message" one takes from the play. If, for example, one essentially defends oneself against the implied indictment of Holloway's narrative by offering genuine sympathy and expressing thanks that things aren't that way anymore, the loud-talker has succeeded in exposing one's refusal of history and can then observe archly, "If the shoe fits, wear it."

In other words, loud-talking is the way August Wilson is *doing* American history in his plays, and especially in *Two Trains Running*, in which loud-talking becomes the vehicle for the play's primary historical theme that much of Wilson's white audience still is unable to locate themselves in the represented stage experience. To put it in the vernacular, "white folks just don't get it." This historical point of *Two Trains Running* is not merely to offer a salutary addition or correction to an already existing American history. Instead the play offers its audience the opportunity to *do* American history by including them as participants in a ritual of signifying(g) through which they can become self-conscious about their odd disconnectedness to a black experience around which, as W.E.B. Du Bois put it, "the history of the land has centered for thrice a hundred years."

—Mark William Rocha, "American History as 'Loud Talking' in *Two Trains Running*," *May All Your Fences Have Gates,* ed. Alan Nadel (Iowa City: University of Iowa Press, 1994): pp. 116–132.

SANDRA G. SHANNON ON THE LEGACY OF MALCOLM X

[Sandra G. Shannon, Professor of English at Howard University, is the author of *The Dramatic Vision of August Wilson* and numerous scholarly articles on both Wilson and Amiri Baraka. In this excerpt, Shannon argues that Wilson's aim is to reinvigorate the now misunderstood mission of Malcolm X.]

Set 1969, *Two Trains Running* (1990) presents the debris of an explosive era in black awareness. Its very premise suggests what happens when there are no heirs to carry on the legacy established by past black activists, too many of whom now exist only as martyrs. Wilson expresses this sense of loss in his play for the 1960s by invoking a familiar football analogy—"going back to pick up the ball": "There's a character in *Two Trains Running* [Aunt Ester] who says 'If you drop the ball, you've got to go back and pick it up. There's no need to continue to run because if you reach the end zone, it's not going to be a touchdown. You have to have the ball'" (interviewed by Bond).

According to Wilson, current generations of blacks seem to have abandoned the hard work and sacrifice of their ancestors, paying only lip service to what was their elders' raison d'être. He also laments the cultural emptiness that plagues black youth. Nowhere is this more obvious than in the commercial bonanza stemming from

Spike Lee's 1992 film Malcolm X. Sweatshirts, caps, and a variety of paraphernalia bearing the familiar "X" have become virtually a uniform for many of the same black youth who appreciate little and know even less about their past. Although Malcolm Little's famous "X" originally signified a disavowal of his so-called white name and a celebration of his African roots, in the hands of moneymakers it also became a faddish craze and an emblem of unreflective militance.

Wilson's theme for *Two Trains Running* addresses the misplaced values of today's youth by imploring them to "go back and pick up the ball." Although its metaphor is borrowed from sport, the theme has extremely serious cultural as well as economic implications for black Americans. In particular, it strengthens Wilson's pleas to them to look to the African continuum as inspiration for their cultural preservation and their continued advancement. It is also an appeal to black Americans to continue to confront white America and to demand that which they deserve as citizens, whether that be equal opportunities for employment, comparable pay, or simple fair and human treatment. In addition to its cultural implications within the context of the play, the simple phrase "going back to pick up the ball" describes the politics of economics—an area in which blacks have historically been cast as victims rather than as benefactors. Even more than cultural redemption, then, *Two Trains Running* is a play about the economic survival of black Americans and the many entrenched oppressive forces with which its characters often collide as they choose among luck, violence, and fair play.

—Sandra G. Shannon, *The Dramatic Vision of August Wilson* (Washington, D.C.: Howard University Press, 1995): pp. 166–167.

KIM PEREIRA ON THE SYMBOLIC DEATH OF THE CIVIL RIGHTS MOVEMENT

[Associate Professor of Acting and Dramatic Literature at Illinois State University, Kim Pereira is the author of *August Wilson and the African-American Odyssey*. In this excerpt, Pereira describes the social landscape of the late 1960s as reflected in the play.]

Two Trains Running is Wilson's first post–civil rights play. The year 1969 was obviously an anxious time in the lives and fortunes of African Americans. The riots and conflagrations that surrounded the death of Martin Luther King, Jr., had left in their wake an uneasy social climate. At the beginning of this play, the characters are awaiting the funeral of one of the neighborhood residents. The death of the "Prophet Samuel," whose funeral arrangements are constantly referred to throughout the play, may be seen, on one level, as an extended metaphor for the temporary, symbolic death of the civil rights movement, for his death follows not long after the deaths of the leaders of the two extreme ends of the movement—Martin Luther King and Malcolm X. The struggle to survive appears to falter, if only for a moment—as the characters contemplate not only the death of the "prophet" but also the city council's renovation project that threatens to tear down their neighborhood—but by the end of the play the journey toward self-authentication continues along new paths through the new social terrain of the post–civil rights movement. This pause in the struggle is made even more poignant by the breakdown of the jukebox in the diner—the music that, for three centuries, helped black people through their darkest periods is now silenced, and, for a Wilson play, this silence is deafening. It is noteworthy that for much of the play Aunt Ester is ill and cannot admit visitors, a further reminder of the fragile link to the past. Thus, the music and the oracle, cultural conduits to the past, are temporarily inaccessible.

Two Trains Running reflects the complex social tapestry surrounding African Americans at the end of the sixties. Many of them no longer lived in abject poverty. There are several references to the trappings of commercial success—Cadillacs, color TVs, jewelry, even property. But there are far more references to crime, guns, and killings. Blacks are fighting back any way they can. Refusing to accept the settlement that the city offers him, Memphis goes to court and is astonished to receive a greater amount than he had expected. Unless they fight and take what is theirs, they are doomed to become like Hambone, who goes insane waiting for justice. Memphis runs a diner but finds his business slackening as the neighborhood starts to disintegrate—the supermarket, two drugstores, the doctor, and the dentist have all gone. "Ain't nothing gonna be left but these niggers killing one another," he says. West discovers the most lucrative job— burying other black people.

Despite the tumultuous times, the spirit of survival among Wilson's characters remains undiminished as they continue to scramble and hope—playing the lottery, stealing if they have to, and working where they can. By the end of the play, Sterling manages to see Aunt Ester, who offers him hope and the promise of love. That same day, the music returns—the jukebox is repaired and, even before Risa plays it, Sterling sings to her in a faltering prelude to the full-blown swells of Aretha Franklin's soulful voice. The odyssey continues.

—Kim Pereira, *August Wilson and the African-American Odyssey* (Urbana and Chicago: University of Illinois Press, 1995): pp. 6–7.

QUN WANG ON HEROISM IN THE PLAY

[Qun Wang teaches at California State University, Monterey Bay. He is the author of *An In-Depth Study of the Major Plays of African American Playwright August Wilson: Vernacularizing the Blues on Stage,* in addition to numerous scholarly journals on American ethnic literatures. In this excerpt, Wang defines true heroism through an analysis of Hambone, Risa, Sterling and Memphis.]

Like Gabriel, Hambone has an idiosyncratic appearance. He does not have many lines in the play and his appearance often seems awkward and inopportune. But Hambone's experience epitomizes the whole history of the relationship between black America and white America. From the Declaration of Independence, to the Emancipation Proclamation, to the Civil Rights Movement, the history of the United States is full of broken promises and betrayals. As one of the characters in *Two Trains Running* who truly possesses the "warrior spirit," Hambone is representative of those who are determined to fight for what they deserve. Clarissa Thomas explains to Sterling:

> Most people don't understand Hambone. That's cause they don't take the time. Most people think he can't understand nothing. But he understand everything

what's going on around him. Most of the time he understand better than they do.

Risa is a waitress who works in Memphis's restaurant. She is nur-
turing, compassionate, and eager to protect the integrity of her sense
of dignity and individuality. In "an attempt to define herself in terms
other than her genitalia," Risa "has scarred her legs with a razor." In
appearance, Risa's action is radical and extreme, but it reveals a personality which is as defiant and resolute as Risa is determined to
make people recognize her true identity. Risa's empathetic feeling for
Hambone stems from the fact that both characters have, in their distinct and idiosyncratic ways, expressed their anger and frustration
with a society which threatens to deprive them of their sense of individual worth and dignity.

The character Sterling Johnson also believes that Hambone and he
"got us a thing going." Sterling represents the redemptive man of
action: similar to what Hambone wants from Lutz, Sterling also
demands his just due from society. After getting out of penitentiary,
Sterling tried very hard to find work. He was laid off by Hendricks
Construction Company because there was not enough work.
Applying at J & L Steel put him in a Catch-22 situation. The company told him he had to join the union before he could work, but
the union told him that he "got to be working before" he "could join
the union." Tired of waiting for changes to occur, Sterling wants to
control his own destiny. He takes it as his responsibility to redress
social injustice. ⟨. . .⟩

Unlike Risa and Sterling whose sympathy for Hambone originates
from their awareness of the similarities in their experience, Memphis
initially does not believe that he and Hambone share anything in
common. A distance is created between the two partly because of the
conflict between Memphis's interest in protecting his business and
Hambone's "inopportune" presence in his restaurant and partly
because of Memphis's conviction that Hambone "let Lutz drive him
crazy." After Hambone's death, however, Memphis begins to develop
an admiration for Hambone's determination to fight for what he
believes in and the tenacity with which Hambone holds onto his
individual principles. Memphis eventually realizes that his demand:
"they got to meet my price!" is, in essence, not very much different
from what Hambone wants from Lutz. ⟨. . .⟩

Indeed, the true heroes in *Two Trains Running* are not people such as Prophet Samuel whose relationship with his followers is as equivocal as how rich they believe he is. The true heroes in the play are ordinary people such as Hambone, Risa, Sterling, and Memphis who have demonstrated a commonality in their struggle to protect their sense of identity and dignity, to gain respect and independence, and to fight for control of their destiny.

—Qun Wang, *An In-Depth Study of the Major Plays of African American Playwright August Wilson: Vernacularizing the Blues on Stage,* vol. 6 of *Black Studies* series (Lewiston, New York and Queenstown, Ontario: The Edwin Mellen Press, 1999): pp. 118–119, 122–123.

Works by
August Wilson

"For Malcolm X and Others." 1969.

"Bessie." 1971.

"Morning Song." 1971.

"Muhammed Ali." 1972.

"Theme One: The Variations." 1973.

The Homecoming. 1979.

The Coldest Day of the Year. 1979.

Fullerton Street. 1980.

Black Bart and the Sacred Hills. 1981.

Jitney. 1982.

The Mill Hand's Lunch Bucket. 1983.

Ma Rainey's Black Bottom. 1984.

Fences. 1985.

The Janitor. In *Short Pieces from the New Dramatists.* Ed. Stan Chervin. 1985.

Joe Turner's Come and Gone. 1986.

The Piano Lesson. 1987.

Two Trains Running. 1990.

"I Don't Want Nobody Just 'Cause They're Black." *Spin.* 1990.

August Wilson: Three Plays. 1991.

"How to Write a Play like August Wilson." *New York Times.* 10 March, 1991.

"The Legacy of Malcolm X." *Life.* December 1992.

"I Want a Black Director." In *May All Your Fences Have Gates.* 1994.

Seven Guitars. 1995.

The Piano Lesson (adapted for television). 1995.

"The Ground on Which I Stand." *American Theater.* 1996.

"Living on Mother's Prayer." *New York Times.* 12 May 1996.

King Hedley II. Premiered 1999 (unpublished).

Works about
August Wilson

Adell, Sandra. "Speaking of Ma Rainey / Talking About the Blues." *May All Your Fences Have Gates.* Ed. Alan Nadel. Iowa City: University of Iowa Press, 1994. 50–66.

Awkward, Michael. "The Crookeds and the Straights: *Fences,* Race, and the Politics of Adaptation." *May All Your Fences Have Gates.* Ed. Alan Nadel. Iowa City: University of Iowa Press, 1994. 204–29.

Baker, Houston A., Jr. *Blues, Ideology, and Afro-American Literature.* Chicago: University of Chicago Press, 1984.

Baraka, Imamu Amiri (see also Jones, LeRoi). *Blues People.* New York: W. Morrow, 1963.

Barnet, Douglas O. "Up for the Challenge." *Forum:* "Plowing Against Wilson's Ground: Four Commentaries on the Cultural Diversity Debate." *American Theater* 13, no. 10 (1996): 60.

Bogumil, Mary L. *Understanding August Wilson.* Columbia: University of South Carolina Press, 1999.

———. "'Tomorrow Never Comes': Songs of Cultural Identity in August Wilson's *Joe Turner's Come and Gone,*" *Theatre Journal* 46, no. 4 (December 1994): 463–76.

Christiansen, Richard. "Artist of the Year: August Wilson's Plays Reveal What It Means to Be Black in This Country." *Chicago Tribune* (27 December 1987): F9–F10.

DeVries, Hillary. "A Song in Search of Itself." *American Theater* (January 1987): 22–25.

Dworkin, Norine. "Blood on the Tracks." *American Theater* (May 1990): 8.

Elam, Harry J., Jr. "August Wilson's Women." *May All Your Fences Have Gates: Essays on the Drama of August Wilson.* Ed. Alan Nadel. Iowa City: University of Iowa Press, 1994. 165–181.

Ellison, Ralph. *Shadow and Act.* New York: New American Library, 1964.

Gates, Henry Louis, Jr. "Department of Disputation: The Chitlin' Circuit." *The New Yorker* (3 February 1997): 44–55.

Gottlieb, Peter. *Making Their Own Way: Southern Black Migration to Pittsburgh, 1916–1930.* Champaign: University of Illinois Press, 1987.

Harris, Trudier. "August Wilson's Folk Traditions." *August Wilson: A Casebook.* Ed. Marylin Elkins. New York and London: Garland, 1994. 49–67.

Harrison, Paul Carter. "August Wilson's Blues Poetics." *August Wilson: Three Plays,* by August Wilson. Pittsburgh: University of Pittsburgh Press, 1991.

Jones, LeRoi (see also Baraka, Imamu Amiri). *Blues People.* New York: W. Morrow, 1963.

Kubitschek, Missy Dehn. "August Wilson's Gender Lesson." *May All Your Fences Have Gates.* Ed. Alan Nadel. Iowa City: University of Iowa Press, 1994. 183–99.

Leverett, James, et al. "Beyond Black and White: 'On Cultural Power': 13 Commentaries." *American Theater* 14, no. 5 (1997): 14–15, 53–56, 58–59.

Lieb, Sandra R. *Mother of the Blues: A Study of Ma Rainey.* Amherst: University of Massachusetts Press, 1981.

McDonough, Carla J. *Staging Masculinity: Male Identity in Contemporary American Drama.* Jefferson, N.C.: McFarland, 1997.

Mills, Alice. "The Walking Blues: An Anthropological Approach to the Theater of August Wilson." *Black Scholar* 25, no. 2 (1995): 30–35.

Moyers, Bill. *A World of Ideas.* New York: Doubleday, 1989.

Nadel, Alan. "Boundaries, Logistics, and Identity: The Property of Metaphor in *Fences* and *Joe Turner's Come and Gone.*" *May All Your Fences Have Gates.* Ed. Alan Nadel. Iowa City: University of Iowa Press, 1994. 86–104.

Palmer, Robert. *Deep Blues.* New York: Viking, 1981.

Pereira, Kim. *August Wilson and the African-American Odyssey.* Urbana and Chicago: University of Illinois Press, 1995.

Peterson, Robert. *Only the Ball Was White: A History of Legendary Black Players.* New York: McGraw-Hill, 1970.

Reed, Ishmael. "In Search of August Wilson: A Shy Genius Transforms the American Theater." *Connoisseur* 217 (March 1987): 92–97.

Richards, Lloyd. "Introduction." *Fences,* by August Wilson. New York: New American Library, 1987. vii–viii.

Rocha, Mark William. "American History as 'Loud Talking' in *Two Trains Running.*" *May All Your Fences Have Gates.* Ed. Alan Nadel. Iowa City: University of Iowa Press, 1994. 116–32.

Saunders, James Robert. "Essential Ambiguities in the Plays of August Wilson." *Hollins Critic* 32, no. 5 (1995): 2–11.

Savran, David. *In Their Own Words: Contemporary American Playwrights.* New York: Theater Communications Group, 1988.

Shafer, Yvonne. "Breaking Barriers: August Wilson." *Staging Difference: Cultural Pluralism in American Theatre and Drama.* Ed. Marc Maufort. New York: Peter Lang, 1995. 267–85.

Shannon, Sandra G. "A Transplant That Did Not Take: August Wilson's Views on the Great Migration." *African American Review* 31, no. 4 (Winter 1997): 659–66.

———. "Blues, History, and Dramaturgy: An Interview with August Wilson." *African American Review* 27, no. 4 (1993). 539–59.

———. *The Dramatic Vision of August Wilson.* Washington, D.C.: Howard University Press, 1995.

Smith, Philip E., II. "*Ma Rainey's Black Bottom:* Playing the Blues as Equipment for Living." *Within the Dramatic Spectrum.* Ed. V. Hartigan Karelisa. Lanham, Md.: University of America Press, 1986.

Steele, Shelby. "Notes on Ritual in the New Black Theater." *The Theater of Black Americans.* Ed. Errol Hill. New York: Applause, 1987.

Wang, Qun. *An In-Depth Study of the Major Plays of African American Playwright August Wilson: Vernacularizing the Blues on Stage. Black Studies* series, vol. 6. New York, Ontario and Wales: The Edwin Mellen Press, 1999.

Werner, Craig. "August Wilson's Burden: The Function of Neoclassical Jazz." *May All Your Fences Have Gates.* Ed. Alan Nadel. Iowa City: University of Iowa Press, 1994. 21–50.

Wolfe, Peter. *August Wilson.* Twayne's United States Authors Series. Ed. Frank Day. New York: Twayne Publishers, 1999.

Index of
Themes and Ideas

BLACK BART AND THE SACRED HILLS, 12

FENCES, 9, 30–53; Alberta in, 30, 31, 32, 37; as baseball game, 30, 31, 32, 33, 36–37; Blues in, 36; Jim Bono in, 30, 31, 32, 34, 37, 38; characters in, 34–35; Cory in, 30, 31, 32, 33, 34–35, 37, 38–39, 42; critical reception of, 12; critical views on, 36–53, 69; Death in, 30, 32, 33, 37–39, 69; Ellison's carpet metaphor in, 42–43; fences in, 31, 32, 36, 38; Gabriel in, 30–31, 32, 33, 34, 37, 56, 69; hope in, 44; Lyons in, 31, 32–33, 34, 37, 45, 46; Troy Maxson as tragic hero in, 43; Troy Maxson in, 30–33, 34, 36–37, 38, 40, 42–43, 44, 45–46, 56, 69; Troy Maxson's psychic strength in, 42–43; Troy Maxson's storytelling in, 30, 31, 37, 45–46; as meta-comedy, 43–44; plot summary of, 30–33; race relations in 1950s in, 30, 31, 36, 39–42, 44; Raynell in, 32, 35, 37; Rose in, 30, 31–32, 33, 34, 36, 37, 38, 44, 45, 56; song of Blue in, 38–39

JITNEY, 12

JOE TURNER'S COME AND GONE, 47–62; African-Baptist conversion pattern in, 47, 50, 58–60; Bertha's kitchen in, 47, 48, 49, 56; Mattie Campbell in, 48, 49, 52, 55–56; characters in, 51–53; critical reception of, 12; critical views on, 9–10, 37, 54–62, 69; Molly Cunningham in, 48, 49, 52; Eugene in, 48, 49; folklore in, 47, 54; Bertha Holly in, 47, 48, 49, 51, 55, 56, 57; Seth Holly in, 47, 48, 49, 51, 57, 58; Jeremy in, 47, 48, 49; "Joe Turner's Come and Gone" in, 49; Juba dance as mode of spiritual healing in, 48, 56, 61–62; "the little me within the big me" in, 10, 58–60; Herald Loomis in, 10, 47–49, 50, 51, 55, 56, 61, 62; Zonia Loomis in, 47–48, 49–50, 52; Miss Mabel in, 49; Reuben Mercer in, 48, 49–50, 52; Martha Pentecost in, 47–48, 49, 50, 52, 69; plot summary of, 12–13, 47–50; religious intensities in, 9–10; Rutherford Selig in, 47, 48, 50, 51, 57, 58, 59; Shamanism of Bertha and Bynum in, 47, 48, 49, 54, 55–57, 57, 62, 69; Shiny Man figure as surrogate God in, 47, 50, 57, 58, 59, 60–61; slave past in, 47, 49, 54–55; storytelling in, 57; Joe Turner in, 48, 49, 53; Bynum Walker in, 47, 48, 49, 51, 54, 55–57, 58–61, 62, 69; white viewers transported into black reality in, 57–58

KING HEDLEY II, 12

MA RAINEY'S BLACK BOTTOM, 9, 14–29; African American themes in, 25–26; band room in, 14, 21, 29; black-white clash of loyalties in,

23–24; Blues in, 15, 23–24, 25–28; characters in, 17–19; control room in, 21; critical views on, 20–29, 41; Cutler in, 14, 15, 16, 17, 22–23, 27; Dussie Mae in, 14–15, 18, 29; as Greek tragedy, 22–23; Irvin in, 14, 15, 16, 17, 23, 24; Levee in, 14, 15, 16, 18, 22, 23, 25, 26, 27, 29; Ma Rainey in, 14–15, 16, 18, 21, 22, 23–24, 25, 26, 27, 28–29; "Ma Rainey's Black Bottom" in, 16, 23–24; Ma Rainey's sexuality in, 28–29; plot summary of, 14–16; Policeman in, 15, 18; Slow Drag in, 14, 15, 18, 22, 27; socioeconomic hierarchies in 1927 Chicago in, 20–21, 27–28; studio in, 14, 21, 27; Sturdyvant in, 14, 15, 16, 17, 22, 23, 24; Swing *versus* Blues in, 26–28; Sylvester in, 14, 15, 18; Toledo in, 14, 15, 16, 17, 22, 26, 27

PIANO LESSON, THE, 12, 37

SEVEN GUITARS, 12

TWO TRAINS RUNNING, 9, 63–78; black female self-hatred in, 63–74, 69–71; black heroism in, 76–78; chance and luckiness in, 63, 65, 68–69; characters in, 66–67; critical reception of, 12; critical views on, 68–78; end of Civil Rights Crusade in, 73–76; Aunt Ester in, 63, 64, 65, 67, 69, 70, 71, 73, 75; Hambone in, 63, 64, 65, 67, 75, 76–77, 78; Holloway in, 63, 64, 65, 66, 68, 70, 71–73, 75, 76–77, 78; Malcolm X in, 63, 64, 65, 70–71, 73–74; Memphis in, 63, 64, 65, 66, 68, 69, 70, 75, 77, 78; plot summary of, 13, 63–75; Prophet Samuel in, 63, 64–65, 70, 75, 78; revolutionary continuity preached to black Americans in, 71–73; Risa in, 63–64, 65, 66, 68, 69–71, 75, 77, 78; Sterling in, 63, 64, 65, 66–67, 68, 70, 71, 75, 76–77, 78; West in, 64, 65, 67, 68, 75; Wolf in, 63, 64, 65, 66, 68

WILSON, AUGUST, biography of, 11–13